ROCK SOLID

RELATIONSHIPS

ROCK SOLID

RELATIONSHIPS

Strengthening Personal Relationships with
Wisdom from the Scriptures

Wendy L. Watson, Ph.D.

DESERET
BOOK

SALT LAKE CITY, UTAH

Library of Congress Cataloging-in-Publication Data

Watson, Wendy L., 1950–
    Rock-solid relationships : strengthening personal relationships with wisdom from the Scriptures / Wendy L. Watson.
        p.   cm.
    Includes bibliographical references and index.
    ISBN 1-59038-186-6 (alk. paper)
    1. Interpersonal relations—Biblical teaching.   I. Title.

BS1199.I55 W37 2003
248.4'89332—dc22   2003019940

Printed in the United States of America   72076-7141
Publishers Printing, Salt Lake City, UT

10   9   8   7   6   5   4   3   2   1

For Ginny and Kathy

*And now, as the preaching of the word had a great
tendency to lead the people to do that which was just—yea,
it had had more powerful effect upon the minds of the people
than the sword, or anything else, which had happened unto
them—therefore Alma thought it was expedient that
they should try the virtue of the word of God.*

—Alma 31:5

CONTENTS

"He that diligently seeketh shall find; and the mysteries of God shall be unfolded unto them, by the power of the Holy Ghost . . . ; wherefore, the course of the Lord is one eternal round."

ACKNOWLEDGMENTS

The love and counsel of many friends and family members have made this book possible.

Thanks to Mom and Dad, who now live on the other side of the veil, for consistently immersing me in *Rock*-solid love and *Rock*-solid faith.

Thanks to those clients with whom I've worked, who against seemingly insurmountable odds have cleared away the debris of their lives by accessing the power that is in the Atonement and turned their rocky relationships into *Rock*-solid ones.

Thanks to my graduate students, who have given me an ever-increasing desire to discover in the scriptures the wisdom that can help all of us become better marriage and family therapists.

Thanks to my lifelong friend Barbara, who read the manuscript on what should have been her vacation and offered such helpful suggestions from her perspective as a young widow with grown children.

Thanks to Jana Erickson at Deseret Book for her vision, hand-holding, hand-delivering, patience, and endurance—all of which reduced my hand-wringing. What a dream you are to work with!

Thanks to Richard Peterson for his editorial work and for so gracefully helping me express my thoughts more clearly.

Thanks to Truman and Ann and Heber and Ardeth for their gentle mentoring, which always invites me to think beyond what I've thought before and consider other ways to build my life upon *The Rock*.

Thanks to Blaine and Kathy and Wayne and Leslie, who show what *Rock*-solid marriages and friendships are all about.

Thanks to my favorite nephew and nieces and their spouses: Brad and Cindy, Karyn and Chad, Cyndi and Ron, Mandy and Troy, and Rebecca—for the *Rock*-solid love they offer me in various ways, including being willing to "experiment upon the word."

Thanks to Brittney, Gabrielle, Tyler, Allison, and Sarah, my great-nieces and great-nephew, who bring me such joy as I hear of their latest childhood antics and from whom I draw strength by looking into their wonderful faces.

Thanks to my favorite brother-in-law, Bryce, for always blessing our family with his *Rock*-solid faith in priesthood power.

Thanks to my *Rock*-solid friends Sheri and Cathy, who are like sisters to me.

And finally, thanks to Kathy and Ginny, who are not only

my sisters but also my friends. Thanks for feeling so confident in our Rock-solid sibling relationships to be able to speak the unspeakable and offer irreverent comments on my early drafts and ideas for this book.

INTRODUCTION

R emember, remember that it is upon *the rock of our Redeemer*, who is Christ, the Son of God, that ye must *build your foundation*; that when the devil shall send forth his mighty winds, yea, his shafts in the whirlwind, yea, when all his hail and his mighty storm shall beat upon you, it shall have no power over you to drag you down to the gulf of misery and endless wo, because of *the rock upon which ye are built*, which is a sure foundation, a foundation whereon if men build *they cannot fall*" (Helaman 5:12; italics added).

What a promise! If, and as, we build our lives upon our Savior Jesus Christ we *will* succeed! In fact, the promise is that no matter what the odds are against us, we "cannot fall." Now, there's a guarantee we can count on!

In a world filled with so much uncertainty, terror, and tragedy we need:

- Places of security

- Commitments we can bank on

- People we can trust

- Love we can rely on

We need *rock*-solid relationships!

Rock-solid relationships are those relationships *that endure* and flourish when the "slings and arrows of outrageous fortune" (*Hamlet* III, i, 56–68) combine with the adversary's storms (see Ephesians 6:12) and the world's alluring sophistries in a relentless and sinister effort to undermine and ultimately destroy love.

ROCK-SOLID RELATIONSHIPS ARE BUILT UPON THE ROCK

So how can we build *rock*-solid relationships? The *only* way is upon *The* Rock, the Rock of our Redeemer. *Rock*-solid relationships, have as their foundation, Jesus Christ. His Power, Light, Love, Truth, and Spirit are their bedrock. Relationships built on these "cannot fall." They just simply can't. They never will—because they are *Rock*-solid.

Rock-solid relationships are built upon *The* Word, who is Christ, and His words, the scriptures. The prophet Nephi, taught, "Feast upon the words of Christ; for behold, the words of Christ will tell you *all* things what ye should do" (2 Nephi 32:3; italics added).

All things?

Yes. *All* things.

How to talk with my teenage son who is suddenly pulling away from us?

How to show love to my wife, so that she really experiences the deep love I have for her?

How to work with my brother on settling our parents' estate, so that our relationship is still alive at the end of the process?

How to respond to my sister—who seems to twist everything I say to her—so that we can be closer?

How to help my seemingly indifferent husband think about my needs sometimes?

How to build a bridge from my heart to my father's and put years of conflict behind us?

How to link arms with my colleagues so that we can accomplish the important tasks at hand and stop wasting our energies on complaints and criticisms, fears and jealousies?

How to be a better wife and mother?

Yes. Absolutely. Certainly. All of these things. As a marriage and family therapist for 30 years, I am convinced the scriptures are *the very* best "how to" books on relationships. The scriptures are the first and last word on how to be a better husband, father, wife, mother, parent, son, daughter, sibling, in-law, friend, neighbor, boss, employee, or any other relationship you can name. The scriptures contain the answers to how to build and strengthen *any* relationship.

Can you imagine there are over a dozen principles for building relationships to be found in just a couple of chapters in 3 Nephi? I can. Because a few years ago with the guidance of the Spirit, I discovered within the account of the Savior's visit to the Nephites principles such as:

- a small voice penetrates positively

- repetition registers truth

- commendations are crucial

- believing and receiving love is beneficial

- pure touch testifies of love

(see Watson, *Purity and Passion*)

Recently I have been intensely focused on helping couples find solutions to problems with their marital intimacy. Once again the scriptures are filled with answers—when we are seeking and seeing with the Spirit. Let me give you just one example. Several verses in Hebrews 13 (1–6; 16) contain magnificent counsel for marriage partners. When these verses are studied with the Spirit and prayerfully pondered, you and your spouse may be convinced that Paul wrote this letter to the Hebrews just for you!

When we don't know the next step to take, when we can't see *any* light at the end of our relationship tunnel, the scriptures—the word of God—are the "iron rod" that we can count on and hold onto. The wisdom contained in the scriptures will guide us over the mountains of misunderstandings, through the dark nights of betrayal, and around the mine fields of destructive traditions and legacies of lethal thoughts, feelings, and behaviors. And all we have to do is be willing to seek their wisdom. "Yea, we see that *whosoever will* may lay hold upon the word of God, which is quick and powerful, which shall . . . lead the man [and woman] of Christ in a strait and narrow course across that everlasting gulf of misery" (Helaman 3:29; italics added)—even that gulf of misery that is created by unhappy and stressful relationships.

WISDOM FROM THE SCRIPTURES
STRENGTHENS RELATIONSHIPS

At the most difficult time in her life, namely, the dissolution of her marriage—because her husband ran off with their young woman boarder—one woman found her daily "to do" list right within the scriptures. Each and every day she took her question for *that* particular day to the Lord in prayer, then opened her scriptures—absolutely expecting an answer—and received abundantly! The scriptures became her personal compass, her very own Liahona, pointing the way she should go through her unexpected wilderness experience (see 1 Nephi 16:10). She discovered in her exploration of the scriptures what Nephi and his family learned about the workings of the Liahona: the more "faith and diligence and heed which [she] did give unto them," the clearer were the instructions she received (see 1 Nephi 16:28).

And she had other experiences that paralleled Nephi's, namely, that what was written in her scriptures was "changed from time to time, according to the faith and diligence which [she] gave unto [them]" (v. 29). At times a passage that she had read many times before suddenly seemed brand new. Other times she found passages that she'd never read; some, she'd never even noticed. It was as though the "scripture angels" were working overtime to insert words and phrases, counsel and advice meant just for her.

Day after day the scriptures told her how to deal with her husband, in the way the Lord wanted, so that her children would not be injured in the crossfire of the rancor of divorce. She was tutored how to heal the fractured relationship with her husband so that, although no longer spouses, they were able to be supportive friends to each other and continue to be great parents to their children.

Because of the marital breakup, this woman needed to seek employment. From her daily seeking in the scriptures, she learned how to present herself at a job interview for a very desirable position within her field. She got the position and then she proceeded, in a very matter-of-fact manner, to take any work-related problem she was not able to solve right to her director—the scriptures—and again received her answers. She figured that since the words of the Lord had helped her get the job, they could now help her do it!

This woman prospered spiritually and temporally. And her relationships prospered. All because of the wisdom from the scriptures, which she diligently sought, found, and applied. This single-parent mother was able to testify to her sons the truth of what Alma told his son: "For just as surely as this director [the Liahona] did bring our fathers, by following its course, to the promised land, shall the words of Christ, if we follow their course, carry us beyond this vale of sorrow into a far better land of promise" (Alma 37:45). Indeed, the words of Christ had consistently carried her beyond her vale of sorrow into a far better land of promise—a land complete with loving relationships.

A CAUTION ABOUT CONTEXT

As a marriage and family therapist I believe that context is crucial. To understand a certain thought, feeling, or action, we need to understand the context. For example, a woman with tears in her eyes might be sad, happy, fearful, or have something in her contact lens! We need to know what else is happening in her life to correctly interpret her tears. So it is with the scriptures. If we take the scriptures out of context, we may at best miss the depth of what they are trying to teach us and at worst come to some erroneous conclusions about how we should act, think, or feel.

For example, a single woman who gets frequent telephone calls from men inviting her on dates, but who never receives a marriage proposal, may quip, comparing her situation with that of her married friends, "Many are called, but few are chosen." That may (or may not) be humorous, but such use of that familiar scripture misses the profound wisdom of D&C 121:34, when considered in its full context.

Here's another frivolous example: If we take what Timothy and Isaiah have to say out of context and combine them, we can justify not exercising and eating whatever we want. How so? Read these two scriptures:

"For bodily exercise profiteth little" (1 Timothy 4:8). You might even add in verse 9 for extra validation: "This *is* a faithful saying and worthy of all acceptation."

Combine that notion with Isaiah's invitation to "Let your soul delight itself in fatness" (Isaiah 55:2), and you've got a divine license to be a couch-potato—but *only* if taken out of context.

Having considered this caution about context, many of us cannot deny the joy that comes when, having labored over a problem and taken it to the Lord in prayer, the Spirit guides us to a particular passage; often, a verse; sometimes, a phrase; and perhaps, even just one or two words of scripture. At that precise moment, the importance of total context and all the information surrounding those words of the Lord seem to fade into the background. The words seem written just for us. For *our* specific context. For *our* specific time. Those scriptures ring more than true. They resound in our minds and lodge in our hearts. They linger with us, positively influencing our thoughts, feelings, and actions.

Imagine the comfort that comes to a father who, grieving the reckless behavior of his wayward son, prayerfully opens the scriptures and finds this comforting assurance, which seems to have been written just for him by Isaiah: "Thou shalt weep no more: he will be very gracious unto thee at the voice of thy cry; when he shall hear it, he will answer thee" (Isaiah 30:19).

This father suddenly feels less alone in his grief. He feels sustained by the hand of the Lord. He knows that his weeping doesn't go unnoticed by the Savior. And that palpable comfort makes all the difference to how he relates not only with his son, but with his wife and his daughter. All his relationships are shored up.

Through the inspired writings of the prophets and the Savior's own words, we are drawn to the Lord and are able to access His love and power. And it is my firm belief that as we apply the revealed principles, we are able to build and fortify our relationships in ways we have previously never thought possible.

IMMERSING YOURSELF IN THE SCRIPTURES

A distinction needs to be drawn between simply reading the scriptures and regularly immersing ourselves in them. In order to become a member of The Church of Jesus Christ of Latter-day Saints, we were immersed in the waters of baptism. That was only a beginning. We have an ongoing need to be repeatedly *immersed* in the truths of the restored gospel, or we will understand and experience only enough to feel guilty— and not enough of the eternal truths to feel joy. Joy comes through immersion. A little sprinkling of the scriptures in our lives will never bring us the fullness of joy that accompanies regular immersion.

Take a moment to think of how some of your relationships might be strengthened if, through your immersion in the scriptures, you found and heeded the wisdom in:

- 3 Nephi 17:5: *"When Jesus had thus spoken, he cast his eyes round about again on the multitude."*

Wisdom: Take time to notice people's reactions to what you've said. Don't be a "hit and run" talker. Be sensitive to how someone is doing after you've conversed with them.

- Luke 2:19: *"But Mary kept all these things, and pondered them in her heart."*

Wisdom: Keep confidences.

The Prophet Joseph Smith taught, "The reason we do not have the secrets of the Lord revealed unto us, is because we do not keep them but reveal them." Could the same be true with our friends and family members? Can our friends and family members trust us to be a confidante? Would they tell us more if we didn't tell so much of what they tell us to others? We need to be like the Prophet, who declared, "I can keep a secret till Doomsday" (Smith, *Teachings*, 195).

- 1 John 4:19: *"We love him, because he first loved us."*

Wisdom: Be willing to take the first step.

You go first. If you want someone to love you, show love to them first! If you want change in a relationship to happen, *you* make some change—*first*.

- 3 Nephi 18:32: *"For unto such shall ye continue to minister; for ye know not but what they will return and repent, and come unto me with full purpose of heart, and I shall heal them; and ye shall be the means of bringing salvation unto them.*"

Wisdom: Be tenaciously loving.

Our reaching out to a family member or to a friend who is struggling spiritually must not be contingent upon their response. We need to act as directed by the Spirit, not as influenced by the response, or non-response, of the one we seek to help. Imagine the liberation! Our actions, our compassion, our love can be independent of how another behaves or treats us.

- D&C 67: 10: "*Strip yourselves from jealousies and fears, and humble yourselves before me, for ye are not sufficiently humble, [then] the veil shall be rent and you shall see me and know that I am—not with the carnal neither natural mind, but with the spiritual.*"

Wisdom: Put jealousies and fears away and increase humility.

Here the Lord sets forth clear instruction of how to get to know Him better. But could the same thing apply in our relationships with others? Are jealousies, fears, and pride blinding us? Imagine the good we might be able to see in others after we strip ourselves of jealousies and fears and humble ourselves.

- Alma 5 (*the entire chapter*)

Wisdom: Take Alma's self-assessment questionnaire and learn the art of asking questions.

In about 40 questions—the number of questions seems to change, depending on the state of our soul—Alma invites us to reflect on our lives. Those reflections can increase our desire and motivate us to bring necessary changes into our relationships. And as we study Alma's art of asking questions, perhaps we can learn how to invite those we love to also have an increased desire to change.

SEEK ROCK-SOLID RELATIONSHIPS BY STUDY AND ALSO BY FAITH

Though we embrace truth wherever we can find it (Smith, *Teachings*, 313), when we've tried everything else and discovered that neither tears nor the wisdom of the world is enough on which to build loving, lifting relationships that will stand the test of time, it's time to look elsewhere. We need to look where the Savior's disciples looked—to Him and to His words. We need to echo Peter when he said, "Lord, to whom shall we go? thou hast the words of eternal life" (John 6:68).

The scripture that led to the opening of this dispensation was, "If any of you lack wisdom, let him ask of God" (James 1:5). There it is. There's the key to getting answers, direction, guidance, and wisdom. Since this is our dispensation, shouldn't we embrace that "opening" scripture as our guide to any and all questions we have?

I believe you will receive all the wisdom you are seeking to help you and your loved ones if you:

- Take your relationship questions to your Heavenly Father in prayer. Confide in Him the *one* question you most need answered through the scriptures *that* day.

- Ask for the Spirit to be with you as you read the word of the Lord. Plead for the Holy Ghost to be with you. Imagine Him being right there by you.

- Open your scriptures and read until you find the answer. I believe you won't have to read very far because the rest of the scripture that opened this dispensation is true: "[God] giveth to all men liberally, and upbraideth not; and it shall be given him. But let him ask in faith, nothing wavering" (James 1:5–6).

A SUGGESTION ABOUT HOW TO USE THIS BOOK

For more than 10 years, I have been researching the answers to this question: "In what specific ways can the wisdom found in the scriptures help strengthen relationships?" I've been drawn to countless chapters, passages, verses, phrases, and words that, if really believed and lived, would fortify any relationship. In fact, I am convinced that if everyone lived the Ten Commandments and the Beatitudes, I would need a new profession!

I have several hopes for you as you read this book. I hope that:

- You'll find success as you experiment on the 14 principles I have identified that can be applied to strengthen your relationships.

- *Rock-Solid Relationships* will whet your appetite for the words of Christ and stimulate you to seek additional answers in the scriptures to your everyday relationship concerns.

- You'll regularly seek the companionship of the Spirit to find even more wisdom for you and your loved ones.

- You'll heed in a very personal way King Benjamin's directive: "And now, if you believe all these things see that ye do them" (Mosiah 4:10). True wisdom involves application.

- You'll have an increasingly irresistible desire (actually, I'll be happy if you're just willing) to, in Alma's words, "experiment upon [the] word" (Alma 32:27). Read the experiments. Try them. Then try them again. And see what happens.

My real hope is that this book will help you in your quest to build *Rock*-solid relationships.

CHAPTER 1

DO ONE SMALL THING

Out of small things proceedeth that which is great.
—D&C 64:33

W hen you have a seemingly overwhelming problem in a relationship, or a problem that has persisted for years, it's natural to think that you need a big solution. However, your answer may be found in the wisdom of D&C 64:33: "Out of small things proceedeth that which is great." Several other scriptures echo this truth: "A very large ship is benefited very much by a very small helm" (D&C 123:16) and "by small and simple things are great things brought to pass" (Alma 37:6). (See also James 3:4; 1 Nephi 16:29.)

A small adjustment in the way we think about something can often bring great changes in our feelings and behavior. For example, viewing a particular food from the perspective of how it will increase our insulin resistance may help us manage our sugary cravings better than all the behavioral reward systems we've set up for ourselves in the past or all the disparaging words with which we've flogged ourselves. Likewise, a small change in our behavior can often make a huge difference in another person's thoughts, feelings, and actions. For example, a man who turns off his favorite TV program and says to his wife, "I'd rather talk with you than watch this" may precipitate a very beneficial "heart attack" for his wife and begin shoring up their marriage. Consider the great effect seven words spoken by Nephi had on his father. "Whither shall I go to obtain food?" (1 Nephi 16:23) Nephi asked, awakening Lehi's memory of who he (Lehi) really was—a prophet of the Lord.

Having lived for years with problems in a relationship, it may be difficult to concede that the solution to our frustration can begin with one small change in the way we think, feel, or act. We might feel foolish for having struggled for so long with problems that could have been solved by a small thing. "You mean it's as simple as that?" may be our initial protest, echoing Naaman's indignation when Elisha prescribed something as easy as bathing seven times in the Jordan river as a cure for leprosy (see 2 Kings 5). But the truth is that small things *can* bring about great changes in our relationships, especially when the seemingly small things catch the attention of a child, parent, friend, sister, or spouse—signalling to them that something is different.

EXAMPLES

Grant and Mary were a physically active couple in their 70s. Six months ago, Mary's 74-year-old sister, Clara, moved in with the couple due to Clara's failing health. Grant and Mary were glad to help. "It's the right thing to do," they said. At the same time, however, they felt a bit resentful because they noticed that the more help they gave Clara, the more assistance she requested and required, even though her physical health, according to the doctors, was steadily improving.

Our beliefs about others influence how we relate to them (see Wright, Watson, and Bell, *Beliefs*). Mary believed that Clara would always need someone to take care of her. Both Grant and Mary feared that Clara had to be "babied" to avoid her becoming upset. The couple came to feel they were being held hostage in their own home. And they were—not by Clara—but by their belief that "caring equals doing for—and doing more and more."

Grant and Mary were weary—bone-weary. Was this how their lives would be for the rest of their days? What could they do? The answer was in D&C 64:33: "Be not weary in well-doing, for . . . out of small things proceedeth that which is great."

That scripture is often quoted to encourage us to continue doing what we're doing. However, the answer for Mary and Grant—and Clara—was to do something *different*, to make some small changes in what they were doing. And out of those "small things," proceeded the "great" relief that Mary and Grant were seeking.

What did they do? What were the small things that helped them "be not weary in well-doing" and brought great relief to the couple while benefiting Clara?

Mary and Grant began to wonder if their *helpfulness* to Clara was unintentionally inviting her to be more *helpless*. They were literally doing everything for Clara. As a result, Clara was doing nothing for herself. And seeing that Clara did nothing for herself only reinforced for Mary and Grant that they *needed* to do everything for her. What a vicious cycle of helpfulness and helplessness!

The couple decided to make one small change. They decided that for one week they would stop pouring Clara's glass of water for breakfast and see how she would respond. What did Clara do? She began pouring her own water. Encouraged by this, the next week while making supper, Mary said wearily, outloud to herself, "I'm so tired. I need some help cutting these vegetables." Promptly, Clara got up out of her chair and started helping Mary. Noticing Clara's response to these two situations, Mary and Grant invited Clara to take more responsibility for herself over the next several weeks. They encouraged her to be more helpful around the house by taking time to show her where clean bed sheets and the toaster were located. Within just three weeks, Clara was helping herself *and* Mary and Grant more—making her own bed, dusting the living room furniture, and making toast for breakfast.

The effect of these "small things" breathed life back into Mary, Grant, and Clara. Clara continued to make steady improvements in taking care of herself and helping with daily life around the home. Mary and Grant were even able to take a trip they had been looking forward to but believed they could never take because of Clara's previous dependency. And all three reclaimed the joy of being together. Several small things—that were different—interrupted the vicious cycle that had for a time trapped them all. The wisdom of "out of small things proceedeth that which is great" strengthened these three individuals and their relationships.

Martha was the single-parent mother of three out-of-control, extremely unhelpful adolescents. In a futile effort to solicit their help, she had resorted to pleading, cajoling, yelling, and making task charts, all of which her children had learned to ignore. Exhausted and discouraged, Martha was on the verge of despair. She was more than "weary" in her well-doing, she was sick and tired of the whole thing! Then one day Martha decided to do something different. Very different. Something that, although "small," was different enough to make a difference.

One night Martha turned the kitchen table upside down (that's how she felt their family life was) and made a picnic on the living room floor. She didn't yell. She didn't plead. She just said, "Dinner's in here" and sat down to eat with her children on a blanket. What resulted from that small (and unusual) thing? The children starting helping. Who knows how that out-of-the-ordinary behavior affected them? Did they think to themselves, "Boy, we'd better start doing something to help Mom, she's going crazy" or "Hey, our Mom is more fun than we thought. She's cool. Let's help her"? Who knows? But the result was that the children started helping, and Martha stopped yelling.

To strengthen the changes in her children's behavior, Martha also did one other "small thing." Feeling badly about all the nagging and complaining she had previously done, she wanted each child to hear her say something positive about them. However, also fearing that her adolescents might discount such comments if she offered them directly—"Oh Mom is just trying to psych us out"—Martha looked for opportunities for them to overhear expressions of her love and admiration. So, while talking with a friend on the telephone or in person, and knowing that her child was within listening distance, she would say, depending on which child was close by:

"I don't know why I'm so fortunate to have a daughter like Janice" or "Jeremy is such a joy to me" or "Tyler is such a great young man." Those commendations caught her children's attention and captured their hearts.

How could such a small comment delivered in such an oblique way make such a difference? Because both Martha's message and her delivery were so *different* from what her children had experienced before. That is, while Martha's previous tone had been harsh and critical when speaking with her children, it was now soft and calm while talking with a friend on the telephone. These expressions were also positive, rather than negative; and they were overheard, rather than delivered directly, which somehow gave them more credibility.

The feelings of appreciation Martha had truly felt deep in her heart but which had gone unspoken for so long, were finally heard, and they spawned a spirit of peace and cooperation where there had previously been only conflict. This family had had a picnic on the living room floor, and the wise mother had made certain her children overheard expressions of her true feelings for them. The changes that took place in that home are yet further proof that "out of small things proceedeth that which is great." A couple of small things had made a very big difference.

EXPERIMENT UPON THE WORD

How can you apply the promise that "out of small things proceedeth that which is great"? (D&C 64:33) Think of one of your relationships that needs help and try to identify what the problem is. Remember that a large part of solving any problem is being able to identify it. A problem without a definition is a problem without a solution. Ask yourself what problem concerns you most in that relationship.

Now, think about the smallest amount of change—in yourself, the other person, or in your relationship—that would indicate that you are making progress. Most of us are tempted to think of large changes, especially when we're craving relief. But, just for a few minutes, rein in those tendencies and really think about one *small* change you would like to see. What could you do, or not do; say or not say; feel or not feel, that would indicate that something is different? For example, "The day I am able to greet my daughter-in-law at the door with a hug, I'll know we're making progress."

Perhaps it is the other person's behavior or words that would catch your attention the most. For example, "The day my dad asks me about my life is the day I'll know things are changing."

Next, consider what small change the *other* person might believe is indicative of progress. What small change in you, or in him or her, or in how you relate would be a minimal litmus test of change, from your loved one's perspective? For instance, would your friend say, "The day we are able to talk about vacation plans, without getting upset, will indicate we're making progress"?

Think back to solutions you have tried in the past to improve this particular relationship. What have you typically done to relieve the situation? Whatever your answer is, it is probably one thing you should *stop* doing! It's been said that "the solution to the problem can become the problem." If you have typically responded to the distressful situation in your relationship by withdrawing—and nothing has changed—it's time to stop withdrawing. If you typically defend yourself—

and nothing is different—stop defending. If moping has been your modus operandi, cease moping. If you want things to be different, try something *different*.

Remember Mary and Grant? They typically did everything for Clara. Then they decided to do something different. One small thing. They stopped pouring her water for breakfast. And that small change initiated great, beneficial changes for all three. Think about Martha and her adolescents and the small changes that brought such great improvements. So, do something different. Do one small thing.

Pray for the Spirit to whisper to you the one "small thing" that would make the biggest difference to your troubled relationship. Perhaps it will be something small that your loved one has previously requested but you have resisted. Then pray to have the strength to do that one small thing. Pray to have the strength to "be not weary" in doing the small things, so that great things—all those things you've longed for in your relationship—will indeed happen.

One woman, who longed for a closer emotional connection with her husband and an increased feeling that he really loved and respected her, read the manuscript of this book. She said, "Well, I guess my heart isn't as open as I thought it was because the only 'small thing' I'm presently willing to do is to give my husband this chapter to read! I want *him* to do 'one small thing' first." If you feel like that woman, take a deep breath and consider the words in Alma 33:21: "If ye could be healed by merely casting about your eyes that ye might be healed, would ye not behold quickly, or would ye rather harden your hearts in unbelief, and be slothful, that ye would not cast about your eyes, that ye might perish?" Paraphrasing this scripture we might ask: If your relationship could be healed or strengthened by merely doing the one small thing that comes to your mind and heart as you prayerfully consider this experiment, would you not do that one small thing quickly? Or would you harden your heart "in unbelief, and be slothful," and resist the small, out-of-the-ordinary thing that would keep your relationship from perishing?

Think again about the power of seemingly small things. For one week, do one small thing—one small thing that is *different*—and watch what great things await.

CHAPTER 2

GIVE THE LOVE YOU
WANT TO RECEIVE

Therefore all things whatsoever ye would that
men should do to you, do ye even so to them.
—Matthew 7:12 (see also 3 Nephi 14:12)

Many feuding husbands and wives, stressed-out parents and children, and alienated friends would be astonished to discover their feelings toward one another are so intricately intertwined that their feelings are almost, if not exactly, identical. These feelings, which could be called "twin feelings," develop over time as the individuals involved interact with each other. Unhappy marriage partners may *each* harbor feelings of loneliness and rejection. Ironically, these husbands and wives are inseparably connected in feeling all alone.

Imagine the difference it might make if we were able to see into the heart of our spouse or child or friend and discover they feel the same unhappiness, concern, fear, and frustration we do. Incredibly, some positive changes can begin to occur by merely seeking to identify if "twin feelings" exist in a relationship. For instance, changes in our thoughts and feelings may start bubbling up, almost unbidden, when we ask ourselves: "What if my spouse (or child, sibling, friend, parent) is feeling as lonely (or underappreciated, or misunderstood, etc.) as I am?"

Is it possible that you share "twin feelings" with someone in your life? Imagine what might happen if you were able to identify such situations and follow the wise counsel offered in Matthew 7:12: "Therefore all things whatsoever ye would that men should do to you, do ye even so to them."

EXAMPLES

Feeling rejected by his wife, a man withdrew from her—physically, emotionally, verbally, and spiritually. He was afraid to reach out to his wife, believing that she would only reject him again. He didn't believe that his breaking heart could manage one more rejection. And he longed for her to reach out to him.

At the same time, yet unknown to him, his wife believed that *he* didn't care about *her* anymore. Fearing rejection, she was afraid to reach out to him, yet she yearned for him to reach out to her.

Their "twin feelings" of rejection and longing for love were coupled with their mistaken "twin beliefs," which also held their relationship captive. The husband believed: "She doesn't like me and doesn't like being with me." In twin fashion, the wife believed: "He doesn't like me and doesn't like being with me."

Their relationship was on a crash course. What could help?

This husband was courageous enough to follow the admonition found in Matthew 7:12. While bracing himself for a giant shot of rejection, and putting his own needs aside, the husband bravely began giving to his wife exactly what he wished to receive from her. He greeted her each morning with a smile—a warm, genuine smile. He began calling her from his work during the day to express appreciation for her and to inquire about her day and how it was going. He hugged her when he returned from work and found frequent, everyday ways to say and show "I love you and am so grateful to have you in my life." Day after day he did for his wife and said to his wife the very things he longed for his wife to do for and say to him.

The result? Their vicious cycle of interaction, which had led each of them to feel rejected and unloved, was stopped dead in its tracks by the husband's actions. Each spouse felt loved and accepted, and their relationship steadily improved.

This husband learned that in situations where intertwined or "twin feelings" exist, it takes only one person who is willing to suspend his or her fears and needs and courageously go where neither have previously dared to tread—to heal *both* parties. He did so by *offering* that which he wished to *receive*.

One note of caution: As we give the love we wish to receive, we need to be exquisitely sensitive to the response of the recipient, which can tell us if we're hitting the mark—the "love mark" in this case. For example, one husband was bewildered when he gave *to* his wife exactly what he wanted to receive *from* her—and nothing changed. In fact, things got worse. What was his "do unto others" gift? A fishing rod!

$\mathcal{L}$❤

Heather, a 28-year-old woman, applied the wisdom of Matthew 7:12 by *sending* the letter she most desired to *receive*.

It was a letter to her younger sister, expressing all the things she longed to receive from her sister but which had been withheld, namely: love, caring, understanding, interest, appreciation, and an invitation to enjoy a closer relationship:

Dear Paula,

I just wanted to write to you and let you know how much I appreciate you. I have loved watching how you have become who you are. You are such a great example in my life in so many ways. I have always longed for a closer friendship with you. I am not really sure how to go about developing one. Sometimes I feel really distant from that goal, but I always long for it and hope for it. Sometimes I feel so alone and unaccepted in our family. I wonder if you feel that way too, at times. I wish I knew how to change that and invite more love and acceptance into our relationship and family.

I remember when we were much younger, we promised one another not to let the other make the same mistakes Mom has, and we promised to be there for one another and help each other. I don't know how we can do this, being so distant. Being there for one another and knowing each other better and caring about one another will help us come through on our childhood promise.

We only live three and one-half hours away from each other. Emotionally I feel we are separated by the Great Wall of China. I long for family loyalty and unity. I long for your friendship, and fear your rejection and criticisms. I wonder if you feel this way too.

Paula, you are wonderful. You have such a pleasant

personality. You are hospitable and give to so many people. I feel I am always learning things I can do better when I am around you. I hope we can find a way to be closer. I would really like that and feel I need it in my life. I hope you do too.

Love, Heather

Heather's letter—one she wished she could have received—triggered a great strengthening of the sibling relationship, and the positive effects continued to ripple through the entire family, culminating in a rare gathering for a family reunion—something that had not occurred in almost a decade.

EXPERIMENT UPON THE WORD

"Therefore all things whatsoever ye would that men should do to you, do ye even so to them" (Matthew 7:12). How can these words strengthen your relationships? Try the following experiment.

Think about a specific relationship you wish were stronger (better, warmer, more enjoyable, more loving, etc.). What are two or three of the most difficult feelings you presently experience in that relationship?

Ponder the possibility that the other person is struggling with the same feelings toward you that you feel toward him or her.

Then ask yourself the following:

What could [my mother, husband, child, friend] do or say that would heal or strengthen our relationship? Phone me? Consider my point of view? Really listen to me? Send me a thank-you note? Apologize to me? Ask me how my day is going? Forgive me? Express gratitude? Say "I love you"? What effect would it have on me if he or she were able to do so? How would it make me feel?

Now, putting aside your own needs and fears, make a commitment to *do for that individual* the one thing you most wish he or she would *do for you*. Speak the words you most want to hear. Give the love you want to receive. Reach out for the hand that you wish would reach out for yours.

For example, you might commit that for one week you will daily express sincere appreciation and gratitude to the other person, because this is the very thing you wish that he or she would do for you.

There is a catch. Don't give what you wish to receive with any expectation of reciprocity—no expectation that the other person will respond to you in kind. This is your opportunity to give with *no* strings attached. To express love, period. To do otherwise would be manipulation. Remember, this is an experiment. An experiment to see if "twin feelings" exist. An experiment to see what happens when you give the love you wish to receive. It's really an experiment in altruism. One where you care more about the needs and feelings of another than your own—but where you use your needs and feelings as initial clues and cues about how to reach out to your loved one. Think of yourself as a scientist. You can't anticipate or predict the outcome. Focus on your desire to "experiment upon the word"— the words of Matthew 7:12—and then stand still, be still, and watch what happens—not to the other person, but to you. Notice how you feel. Then, consider what else you wish the other person would do for you—and once again, do it for him or her. Watch your feelings and your relationship soar. That really is one distinct possibility when you give the love you want to receive.

CHAPTER 3

WATCH YOUR THOUGHTS ABOUT OTHERS

For as he thinketh in his heart, so is he. —Proverbs 23:7

Think about this proverbial truth: As we think in our hearts, so are we. Does that thought about *our thoughts* catch your attention? When you consider the truth that *everything* you think is registered at the cellular—and at what could be called the "soul-ular"—level, does it make you want to be a bit more careful about the thoughts you entertain? When you consider that you can actually raise or lower your blood pressure just by thinking certain thoughts, think about the effect thoughts might be having on your spirit.

Over time, we become more and more like the thoughts that fill our minds and stay in our hearts. If our thoughts are filled with light and truth, our very bodies will be filled with light and truth (see D&C 88:67). If our thoughts are filled with darkness and lies, so will we be. We become our thoughts.

We *are* our thoughts. Indeed, as a man (or a woman) thinketh in his heart, so is he.

Let's take it a step further. It's equally true that *our* thoughts about others influence *them!* In fact, we could say: As a man thinketh in his heart *about his wife*, so is *she*. As a woman thinketh in her heart *about her son*, so is *he*.

Does that surprise you? Does it seem impossible that your thoughts about your parents, children, friends, siblings, in-laws (and out-laws) influence *them*, as well as you? Is it difficult to believe that your thoughts about others affect their view of themselves, their feelings about themselves, their aspirations, their dedication, and their determination? That how you define them infiltrates their very being? Could your "ill" thoughts about your spouse actually make him ill? One husband realized that his "ill" thoughts about his wife were having exactly that effect!

EXAMPLE

Diane was deeply troubled about her daughter, Rachel.

Rachel's friends were having a bad influence, and Rachel was slipping into behaviors that were alarming and unaccept-able to her mother. But the more Diane tried to intervene, the more withdrawn Rachel became. Diane complained, "I just can't reach her. She won't eat any meals with us as a family. She won't help with any chores around the house. She's pretty good about coming home on time, but she'll never tell me where she's been." Diane felt that she'd tried every approach—restrictive, lenient, warm, cold, interested, uninterested—in her effort to do something that would help Rachel, but to no avail. Was there anything else she could do?

"I don't have the energy to talk with her," Diane told a

friend. "We only fight anyway. So don't tell me to talk to her, I can't. Basically we can't even be in the same room together without getting on each other's nerves. That's how bad it is."

Diane was out of ideas, out of energy, and out of hope. Or so she thought, until she started to *think about her thinking*. Things started to change the day that Diane realized how many negative thoughts she was having about Rachel. Though she loved her daughter and wanted only good things for her, Diane realized, "I don't really *like* my daughter. I think of her as weak, deceitful, and cruel. From time to time I try to reach out to her, but in my heart I only think negative, horrible things about her most of the time."

Could it be that Diane's "negative, horrible" thoughts about Rachel were registering in *Rachel's* cells and spirit and contributing to her "negative, horrible" behavior? Previously, Diane had only thought about it in the reverse, i.e. that it was Rachel's behavior that influenced what Diane thought about her daughter. However, Diane was willing to consider anything. Anything, that is, that might relieve the tension and conflict in her relationship with her daughter. In that spirit, Diane started to examine her thoughts about Rachel. She couldn't believe what she found. She discovered that she had fallen into a pattern of continually comparing her daughter to herself (Diane) or to her other children, with Rachel always coming up short. She frequently reflected: "I never would have acted like that at her age," "She's not like any of my other kids," and on very distressing days, "Why am I stuck with having a daughter like Rachel?"

Diane was stuck all right—stuck in her "negative, horrible" thoughts about her "negative, horrible" daughter.

Diane thought long and hard about a question posed to her

by a friend: "If you were to discover that what you think about your daughter has a direct and palpable effect, not just on you, but upon *your daughter's* thoughts and feelings about herself, and even upon her actions, would there be anything you would want to change about your thoughts?" This question intrigued Diane and also infused her with some energy and hope, for though she didn't have the energy to talk to Rachel, she *did* have the energy to think about her daughter—she was doing that anyway.

Diane knew the kinds of thoughts she would like to have about Rachel. That was easy. She wanted to think of her daughter in positive, hopeful, and loving ways. So Diane began focusing on Rachel's true and eternal identity—a noble, spiritually begotten daughter of God, chosen to experience her mortal probation in these latter days in Diane's home and family. Things did not immediately improve, and some days were more difficult than others. But as Diane was able to more fully embrace this fundamental truth about her daughter, it began to influence the way she viewed Rachel. She started to remember things from Rachel's childhood that revealed her daughter's true spirit—such as her love for people and her great leadership ability. Diane hadn't thought about these things for years. How had she forgotten them? She felt drawn to pull out pictures of Rachel as a child and look at them. There was her Rachel, all smiles. Oh, how she missed those smiles! Diane felt surges of compassion for Rachel as she remembered difficult situations her daughter had faced as a child, and how vigorously and independently Rachel had taken on those troublesome situations.

Over time, Diane's continued efforts to have truth- and light-filled thoughts about Rachel were rewarded again and again.

Some days it seemed that Diane couldn't keep up with new and renewed thoughts about Rachel that poured into her heart and mind. Diane was thrilled. She had finally discovered something she could do for her daughter: She could think truth- and light-filled thoughts about Rachel—over and over again.

No matter how "negatively and horribly" Rachel behaved, Diane persisted. She thought about her daughter's courage, her capacity to love others, her honesty, and her competent ways. She envisioned her positive thoughts serving as a beacon for Rachel, guiding her daughter back to real truths—eternal truths—about herself. Other days Diane thought of her thoughts as a lifeline thrown out to her daughter, reeling her back to safety.

Diane's truth- and light-filled thoughts had a profound effect on *Diane*. She began to feel a loving connection to Rachel, a connection that had eluded her for several years. "I feel like her mother again. These new thoughts about my daughter seem to be giving birth not only to a new Rachel, but to a new me as her mother."

Just as Diane's old "negative, horrible" thoughts had "leaked out" through her words and actions and had a negative effect on Rachel, Diane's new view of her daughter's identity was now having a positive effect. It was as though Rachel could see her reflection in the mirror of her mother's mind and was beginning to respond to that improved image. Where Rachel had been sullen, rebellious, and withdrawn, she was beginning to be more open, happy, and voluntarily involved with the family. Diane also noticed that *she* was herself becoming more and more like the very truth- and light-filled thoughts she was having about her daughter!

Now, did Rachel and Diane ever clash again? Of course

they did. But deep in Diane's heart—registered right there in her cells and in her soul—were thoughts about her daughter that influenced both of them to hang on, to keep trying, to keep talking to each other, and to reach out.

EXPERIMENT UPON THE WORD

Are you ready to experiment upon the words that "as he [or she] thinketh in his heart, so is he"? (Proverbs 23:7) Are you ready to experiment upon the related truth that as we think in our hearts *about others,* so are *they?*

Think of one of your relationships that needs strengthening. Could the other person be reading your mind? That is, could your thoughts about that person be influencing him and your relationship?

Start where Diane started—with your present thoughts about this person. Watch your thoughts. Think about your thoughts. What negative thoughts are you presently having about him or her?

You may feel that your thoughts aren't really negative. If *negative* is too strong a word to describe your thoughts, then ask yourself if your thinking is unintentionally undermining your relationship or tends to put a strain on the way you feel about this person. Be honest. What are the thoughts you have about him or her that may be influencing not only *your* cells and soul, but *his* cells and soul—*his* view of himself, *his* feelings, *his* actions?

Take your time. If you choose to write your thoughts down, put what you've written in a safe place and let it "cool" for a few days before revisiting the list to determine if you have even more negative thoughts to acknowledge.

This is not a pleasant activity. It's typically not a great

experience to fully acknowledge the "negative, horrible" thoughts we've had about others. But if the thoughts are there, the wisdom in Proverbs 23:7 tells us that your thoughts are influencing both of you and your relationship, so let's get them out in the open. Determining our negative thoughts is the first step toward using our thoughts in constructive ways to build relationships. So, be thorough. Look for core destructive thoughts and their tentacles that lead to more. What do you notice about these negative thoughts and their effect on you, on the other person, and on your relationship?

Now, after taking a "super-sleuth" approach to old, past, negative thoughts, it's time to shift your thinking. It's time to "change your mind!" Pray to have truth- and light-filled thoughts about the person brought to you by the Spirit. One woman simply prayed: "Please fill my mind with truths about my brother." She discovered that when she added fasting to her prayers, truths about her brother started to lodge in her heart. She experienced a change of mind *and* a change of heart about her brother.

It's quite possible that the thoughts that come to your mind as and after you pray may be the most accurate thoughts you've had about the other person in a long time. When we are drawn to think something marvelous, amazing, or wonderful about someone else, we are probably closer to acknowledging his or her true self than at any other time. So, pray to be influenced by the Spirit, to have eyes to truly see, and a mind to conceive the wonderful things about this other person. Ask yourself, "When I'm with him or her, in whose presence am I really?" Notice what additional truths come to your mind.

Now, let's try on some of those positive new thoughts. Start by entertaining these new thoughts a couple of times a day, for a day or two, when you are not in the other person's presence. Think right out loud. See how it feels.

Next, find an opportunity to be in the same room as the other person. You don't have to be sitting by them or even in eyeshot. You can each be doing a separate activity. Just be in the same room. Now, think the new thoughts about him or her again. If you need your list to prompt you, take it and review it. Over and over again, while you are in the same room, let those thoughts roll over in your mind. Perhaps a couple of your new thoughts will begin to take root in your heart.

The next step is to sit beside the other person—on the couch, at the dinner table, at church, in the car—and once again go over in your mind those wonderful truths about him or her. You don't need to say a word. Just savor these new truths and watch what happens.

Now, see if you can add any—preferably all—of the following light-filled thoughts to the very specific truths you have already uncovered or remembered about this person. But first, let's take a moment for a brief aside: If you bump up against some particularly dark days where it just seems impossible to think any of the following, take a deep breath, take a little break, and go back to the fundamental truth that the person you are striving to love is a spiritually begotten child of God and has a spark of divinity in him or her. Go back through the process we've talked about previously, and then attempt the following thoughts once again. Don't flog yourself when you hit such a "bump," just start looking for moments—literally one single moment—when you can feel the truth of any one of the following.

Now, here are the light-filled thoughts to rehearse. Notice

what happens when you sit beside your parent, sister, friend, spouse, son, or daughter-in-law, and think *deeply:*

> I . . . love . . . you.
> I love being with you.
> You are a remarkable person.
> I am so blessed and fortunate to have you in my life.
> I believe you have a wonderful mission to perform.
> I admire you and believe in you.

Say the words *slowly* in your mind. Say them over and over again with feeling. Pray to have the truth and power of those thoughts "written . . . in fleshy tables of [your] heart" (2 Corinthians 3:3).

Try this once a day, every day, for seven days. Then try it for another seven. Seven more, and you'll probably have a permanent new etching on your brain and in your heart. You don't have to say a word out loud, just *think* these powerful, healing, truth- and light-filled words. Then, notice what happens. Has something changed? Do you feel differently toward this person? You may be amazed at what you experience. You may even stand in awe as you observe the changes that occur in yourself, the other person, and your relationship—just through entertaining loving thoughts about others.

CHAPTER 4

BURY YOUR WEAPONS OF WAR

They buried their weapons . . . of war, for peace.
—Alma 24:19

I f we have been hurt in a relationship, we often gather an "arsenal of weapons," thinking they will protect our hearts from further damage. But, ironically, such weapons can injure *us* in addition to those we are defending against. These "weapons of war" are thoughts, feelings, and behaviors—such as harsh judgments, jealousies, and sarcasm—that keep us feeling separate, isolated, and lonely. If you are unable to find love and peace and joy in your relationships, could it be you are carrying around thoughts that wound love? feelings that bruise peace? actions that kill joy?

The only thing that these "relationship weapons of war" protect us from is developing loving, lasting relationships. The use of these defensive weapons can make it almost impossible for us to build open, close, caring, supportive relationships.

When we are weary of fighting with others and of not feeling loved and appreciated, perhaps it's time to do as the converted Lamanites—the Anti-Nephi-Lehies—did. Alma 24 contains a stirring account of these remarkable people who so desired a permanent change in the way they related that they were willing to, and did, rid themselves of anything that might wound their brothers—brothers who, by the way, were coming to kill them.

When we are finally ready to enjoy true love and peace and joy in our relationships, we need to be like the Anti-Nephi-Lehies who "buried their weapons . . . of war, for peace." We need to gather our swordlike thoughts, feelings, and behaviors and "bury them deep in the earth" (Alma 24:19, 16).

EXAMPLES

Don, a married father of six grown children, wanted to establish a closer connection with them. His children were polite, but he didn't feel close to them and guessed that they felt the same way. "I've been busy with work all their lives, but that's not the real reason for the distance. I've had a bad temper and have used it against them—against us all, really," he admitted. Like the converted Lamanites, he had become "convinced concerning the wicked traditions of [his] fathers" (Alma 23:3), who had also ruled their families by coercion and fear.

Don was ready to build relationships of genuine love and trust with his children. He started by identifying his "weapons of war"—his impatience, anger, and harsh demands—that had damaged his family relationships. He was able to acknowledge that these were things that had offended and alienated his children over the years.

Then he specifically thought about each child. Don considered his eldest daughter, Jill, and asked himself, "What have I done that has hurt my daughter's heart the most?"

Almost every word of that question stung. *"What have I done?"* Those were words that Don had rarely asked himself in 65 years. He had always been quick to point out how someone else was at fault when difficulties arose. Taking responsibility for his part in problems had never been one of his strengths, and now he could see that same characteristic in a couple of his children.

It grieved Don to consider the second part of the question, " . . . *that has hurt.*" As a child, he had experienced deep emotional pain because of his ungainly, large stature. And, unfortunately, he knew what it felt like to hurt others. Sometimes, driven by his own anguish, he had taken an almost sinister delight in bringing pain to another child.

Then came the next phrase of the question, " . . . *my daughter's heart.*" To think about Jill's heart even for a moment brought Don to tears. He remembered the thrill of first hearing her heartbeat over 40 years before when the doctor had invited him to listen to Jill's fetal heartbeat through a stethoscope. What had he done to that precious heart? How had he wounded it, and filled it with fear and self-doubt?

As Don considered the final part of the question, " . . . *the most,*" he almost groaned. Would he be able to identify *all* the weapons of war he had used in his relationship with Jill? He needed to focus on the ones he thought had done the most damage. What were his most lethal weapons?

Don prayed for strength and guidance to answer. Then to help him focus even more, he asked himself:

What thoughts of mine about Jill, about myself, about life, and so on have bruised her?

What festering feelings have built a barricade between us?

What actions or inactions of mine have almost destroyed our relationship?

The task of identifying his weapons of war was more difficult to do than he initially thought. This wasn't some sanitized list of behaviors, thoughts, and feelings that he could crank out in an hour, and then walk off into the glow of a loving father-daughter relationship with Jill. Time, sweat, and tears would be required. This was hard labor, as intense as the physical labor he was used to. He discovered that working to eliminate anguish and remorse takes a lot of energy. For days he reviewed the past, including missed opportunities to commend Jill, harsh words he regretted ever thinking—let alone saying to her, angry feelings toward her that he had chosen to nurture in his heart.

Don's intense effort to rectify the past paralleled that of the Anti-Nephi-Lehies who proclaimed, "*It was all we could do* to repent sufficiently before God that he would take away our stain" (Alma 24:11; italics added). Indeed, *it was all Don could do* to identify all the weapons of war that he had used against his daughter. He agonized and wept, repented and resolved.

The following are some highlights from Don's soul-searching.

Weapons I've used against my daughter and our relationship:

I tell myself that she doesn't like me and is embarrassed to have me as her father.

I convince myself that I'm just not very loveable.

I focus on how misunderstood, used, and abused I feel as a father.

I rehearse past situations where I feel she didn't respect my authority.

I think how easy her life is compared to how difficult mine was at her age, and I choose to feel resentful about the difference.

I look for ways to bring up situations from her youth in front of other people in order to embarrass her.

I use sharp, cutting words when I speak with her.

I don't really "converse" with her. I'm always on guard to defend my "correct" position, so I never really listen to her.

I find fault with whatever gift she gives me.

I insult her.

I argue with her.

I punish her for mistakes she made as a child or teenager by poking fun at her—but it's always "fun" with a barb attached.

I make her beg me for financial assistance and then make her feel guilty for asking, even though my wife and I have "enough and to spare."

I point out times she has been a disappointment to me as a daughter—sometimes subtly, sometimes not so subtly.

I don't take an interest in her and what's happening in her life right now.

I never let her know how proud I am of her and all she has accomplished in her life.

I never tell her that I love her.

I never tell her that she can always count on me to stand by her as her father and to help her in whatever way I can.

Identifying the weapons he was accustomed to using changed Don. For one thing, it opened his eyes; he couldn't believe he had done all these things; but there they were, right there in black and white and in his own handwriting. The phrase "broken heart and contrite spirit" suddenly had a new and very personal meaning for Don, and he was ready to bring both to the building of a new relationship with his daughter.

Shelly and Trevor were ready to bury their weapons of war. Their marriage had been stuck in neutral for the past ten years, and they wanted a fresh start. As a crucial first step in building a brand-new relationship, they agreed to each make a list of the weapons they had used to wound each other. To do so, they each asked themself, "What are the things I do that keep me feeling lonely and misunderstood in our marriage?" and "What specific 'weapons' do I use that keep me from truly uniting my soul with my spouse?"

They felt it important to identify the weapons of war each had used and to look at the situation from both of their perspectives. They agreed to list:

Weapons of war I have used against myself, my spouse, and our relationship

Weapons of war my spouse will say I've used against myself, my spouse, and our relationship

Weapons of war my spouse has used against himself (or herself), me, and our relationship, and

Weapons of war my spouse will say that he or she has used against himself (or herself), me, and our relationship.

During this experiment Shelly and Trevor learned that it was tempting to use *other* weapons while trying to be self-reflective about *past* weapons. For example, Shelly discovered if she wasn't careful, she drifted almost automatically into thinking negative thoughts about Trevor's approach to the experiment. Thoughts such as the following would come to her mind: "I know that I'll be far more open about disclosing my weaknesses than he'll be" and "I'm sure Trevor will never own up to all the weapons he uses against me and our marriage." Noting these pejorative thoughts allowed Shelly to identify one of her major weapons—namely, believing that she always worked harder in the relationship than Trevor. She realized that her unwillingness or inability to see Trevor's efforts was another destructive weapon of war.

Trevor found himself blaming Shelly for making him use his weapons. For example, almost every time he identified and wrote down one of his weapons of war, he would think: "Well, I wouldn't be using this weapon if Shelly didn't use her weapon of _____." Blaming others for your behavior is itself a very destructive weapon of war.

Trevor also had to be careful that he didn't turn thinking and writing about his weapons into yet another opportunity to criticize Shelly. For example, he found himself writing: "I have negative thoughts about Shelly always being late, about her inability to keep things organized, set priorities, lose weight. . . ." Criticizing others or pointing out another's flaws and imperfections, either to yourself or to them, is another lethal weapon.

EXPERIMENT UPON THE WORD

Think about one of your relationships that needs shoring up. Are you ready for a new relationship with this person? Are you ready to cease sleeping upon your swords (see Ether 15:22)? Are you ready to lay down the weapons of war that have kept you and your loved one feeling disconnected and unloved?

For a moment, really think about the scripture: "They buried the weapons of war, for peace." You are preparing to do battle against weapons that have undermined the building and strengthening of your relationship. This is a very serious undertaking, hardly for the faint of heart, but absolutely necessary for those concerned about the state of their heart.

If possible, discuss this experiment with your loved one. If it's not possible, you can still move ahead.

Start by thinking in general about all the weapons you have used in warring against yourself, against your loved one, and against your relationship. Perhaps reviewing Don's list (in the first example) will trigger your thinking. Remember that your loved one will have the list of weapons he's used.

Remember that these weapons of war are thoughts, feelings, and actions that have kept you separate, lonely, and isolated within your relationship. What weapons have prevented your loved one from knowing your heart?

Consider the irony that our weapons of defense often inflict wounds upon us. Can you think of a weapon that you thought would *protect* you, but has actually *hurt* you? How many self-inflicted wounds do you have?

Continue thinking, and hopefully writing, about your weapons of war. Note that this experiment is not about blaming yourself or your loved one. It's about seeing how, in your best efforts to protect yourselves, you have *each* held back and stifled the growth and development of your relationship. This is the time to start identifying those weapons so that you are not caught off guard should one of those weapons "go off." With the list in hand, you are prepared if a weapon is fired unintentionally. At that point you can say, "That's another thing I do to wound myself, or to wound my loved one and our relationship"—and you can add it to your list of weapons.

Note that it will take time to complete your lists of weapons. This is not a 30-minute activity. It may take 30 days until you feel as though your list is complete. But each time you identify another weapon, you have taken another step forward.

Keep adding to your following lists:

What thoughts or beliefs about myself, about my spouse, about life, love, and so on have I been using as weapons of war? For example: "My belief that I'm really not capable of an intimate, loving relationship is like a spear that pierces my spouse's and my hopes."

What feelings about myself, about my spouse, about life, love, and so on have I been using as weapons of war? For example: "Loneliness is actually a shield I use to keep my spouse at a distance."

What actions—or non-actions—toward myself or my spouse have I been using as weapons of war? Actions also include words spoken. For example: "When I say to my husband that he'll never be able to understand who I really am and what I'm really feeling—those words are just as much a barricade to our marital intimacy as when I consistently interrupt him when he's trying to talk."

After you've identified your weapons of war, order them by rank, using the following criteria:

Which ones do you think have done the most damage to your relationship in the past? To your hearts?

Which one do you think is presently hurting you the most, your loved one the most, and your relationship the most?

Decide which weapon(s) you are ready to lay down, to never use again, to "bury." (Note: Burying even one weapon of war is a great conquest.) Then, consider which ones you are not presently prepared to give up. Ask yourself, "What would need to happen for me to be willing to bury these weapons, to really lay them down and never use them again?"

Now, what can you do with your lists?

a) Keep them in a safe place and review them from time to time in order to add to them as you increase your ability to acknowledge other weapons that you use.

b) Share them with your loved one—only after you have reviewed your weapons, ensuring that they are written in a way that gives *you* more responsibility for the problems than your loved one. (Otherwise you're being like Trevor in the second example.)

c) Talk with your loved one about which weapons you are ready to lay down, to never use again, to "bury."

d) Talk with your loved one about what would need to happen for you to be willing to bury the other weapons.

e) Literally bury your list of weapons—perhaps in a special box as one mother and daughter did—so that if you are ever tempted to use your weapons again, you will have to go and dig them up!

f) Consider what the Anti-Nephi-Lehies did after they buried their weapons of war and were attacked by the Lamanites. Rather than resist, they "prostrated themselves before them to the earth, and began to call on the name of the

Lord" (Alma 24:21). These people were so committed to their pledge to lay down their weapons of war and all the excuses that went with them that they were willing to give up their lives rather than give up their determination.

What might happen if you were similarly motivated? Think of the power that can come to you as you humble yourself before your loved one and the Lord. Think about the increased strength to give and receive love that you will gain as:

You fully acknowledge to your loved one the pain you've caused him or her and the damage you've done to your relationship

You gratefully acknowledge the Lord's help in opening your eyes to the truth

You are willing and prepared to offer no resistance, no excuses, no defenses—even if your loved one initially responds to your efforts by attacking you.

And what might be the outcome as we bury our weapons and refuse to pick them back up? Let's look once again to our Book of Mormon brothers:

"Now when the Lamanites saw that their brethren would not flee from the sword, neither would they turn aside to the right hand or to the left, but that they would lie down and perish, and praised God even in the very act of perishing under the sword—

"Now when the Lamanites saw this they did forbear from slaying them; and there were many whose hearts had swollen in them . . . , for they repented of the things which they had done.

"And it came to pass that they threw down their weapons of war, and they would not take them again" (Alma 24:23–25).

The Anti-Nephi-Lehies buried their weapons, prayed for forgiveness, and didn't offer any resistance when attacked. The outcome was that many of their enemies felt sorry, repented of their cruelty, and threw down their own weapons.

Think what might happen to you, your loved one, and your relationship as you bury your weapons of war.

CHAPTER 5

THERE'S MORE TO GIVING THAN MEETS THE EYE

She . . . cast in all that she had. —Mark 12:44

H e never pulls his weight."

"You'd think with all her talent and time on her hands she would be doing more with her life."

"You can never count on him to do what he says he'll do. He always gets sick or something."

"Can you believe how little she does to help out with Mom? She sure doesn't help like you and I do."

Sound familiar? Such judgments regarding the quantity or quality of another's contribution or participation would probably never be spoken if we had been at the treasury the day the Savior taught his disciples the folly of judging a person's contribution by only looking at what they give. After observing the widow cast in her two mites, Jesus said, "This poor widow hath cast more in, than all they which have cast into the treasury: For all they did cast in of their abundance; but she of her want did cast in all that she had, even all her living" (Mark 12:43–44).

Here's a quick quiz: Who gave more to a family gathering?

a) Marilyn, who brought a plain green gelatin salad, or

b) Brian, who brought all the steaks?

Can we ever really know? Perhaps Marilyn gave more because she wanted to make a special treat for her ailing father whose favorite dessert is green gelatin. Maybe her dad had not been able to attend a family gathering in a long time and she wanted him to have something that she knew he would eat. It's possible she didn't really have the time or energy to make green gelatin that day, and it would have been far easier and faster to buy something. Instead, she gave her last ounce of energy to make the green gelatin for her dad.

Perhaps Brian gave more because he lost his job last week and was feeling depressed and hopeless. His preference might have been to stay home and watch football because everything was an effort for him—even getting out of bed some days. But since his wife had been looking forward to seeing her relatives, he was willing to go. He thought about not taking any food; no one would notice or care. Then he remembered the prime steaks he had purchased last month when he still had a job. He had frozen them, planning to save them for a special occasion. But he decided to use them for this gathering as a way of showing his love and gratitude to his wife and her family.

Or perhaps the scenario is completely different. Maybe Marilyn gave less because she had spent all her money on shoes last week. Then when she was trying to figure out what to make for the family gathering, bemoaning the entire time that she had signed up to bring a dessert, she realized she had some boxes of green gelatin in the pantry. She reminded herself that she didn't really care much for these people and that they didn't like her. Voila: green gelatin!

Maybe Brian gave less because ten months ago he decided to remove red meat from his diet. Yesterday he remembered the case lot of beef that he'd purchased on sale a year ago at the urging of his wife. Wasn't it about time they used those steaks? He was going fishing soon and would need the freezer space to hold his catch. Hence, the stack of steaks for the family gathering.

It simply isn't possible to tell who gave the most without knowing the whole story.

And the truth is that we can never really know the whole story because the whole story includes everything, from what else is happening in a person's life—for example: spiritually, physically, emotionally, socially, financially—to what is happening in a person's heart, which is where the Lord looks—"for man looketh on the outward appearance, but the Lord looketh on the heart" (1 Samuel 16:7).

What *is* someone capable of giving in a particular situation? Again, there are so many factors that come into play, including which commodity is needed. Some family members seem to have a larger capacity for understanding or providing a listening ear. Others may have a greater capacity to offer ideas, financial resources, or hospitality.

What if your capacity to listen and empathize is greater than your sister's? Does that mean that she doesn't love you when she has "cast in all (the listening and empathy) she has," even though her offering is less than you needed and expected? What if your brother's capacity for solving difficult problems is greater than yours? Does that mean he doesn't need and appreciate your input when you "cast in all" that you have?

All that is required to nurture a relationship is to give all we are presently capable of giving, and to treat others as if they are doing the same.

We need to cut others some slack. We need to believe, and show through our actions that we believe, that others are bringing their very best and giving their all—all that they *presently* can—to the "party," just as we are.

Remember, there is great strength in diversity. What if every person in your family and all your friends were exactly the same, and therefore participated in your life in exactly the same way? Consider the words of Paul: "If the whole body were an eye, where were the hearing?" (1 Corinthians 12:17). There are many ways that family and friends can participate and contribute in each other's lives. We need eyes, ears, knees, and toes. For the "whole" to work well, it's actually better that various people do various things. Listen to what the Lord said: "The body hath need of every member, that all may be edified together, that the system may be kept perfect" (D&C 84:110). However, when we compare and criticize the contributions of others, our refrain seems to be: "Give like I give," "Love like I love," "Participate like I participate with our children, with our parents, with our friends, in the Church, in the world."

Isn't that the point of view that got Martha in trouble when she said (in essence): "Mary should take care of the Savior the way I'm taking care of Him. Look at me. I'm cooking and cleaning. Isn't that the mark of a great hostess and of someone who truly cares about His well-being? Look at Mary. She's loafing around. She'll do anything to avoid helping in the kitchen. Why can't she be more like me?"

What a waste of our time and energy, and of the precious resources in our relationships, when we demand of others: "Contribute the way I'm contributing," "Use your talents (which, by the way, should be the same as mine) the way I'm using mine," "Do as I'm doing—follow, follow me!"

Imagine what could happen in a family if individuals were to seek out, celebrate, and capitalize on the differences in their abilities. Consider a family in which one brother struggles financially but is strong spiritually; another brother struggles spiritually but is a great mechanic and computer whiz; one sister struggles with her social skills but is brilliant with managing finances; and another sister is technologically challenged but shines socially. Think of what could happen if "they [would] all labor, every man according to his strength. And they [would] impart of their substance, every man according to that which he [has]" (Alma 1:26–27). Among these four siblings, spiritual, financial, mechanical, computer, and social strengths are available to assist with the spiritual, financial, technological, and social weaknesses that are present. Think of how these siblings' struggles would lessen and their successes increase if the siblings were able to think and work synergistically instead of separately.

Just imagine what could happen if each sibling viewed the family as a pool of resources to which they could contribute and draw from. Instead of being irritated and annoyed by others' "deficiencies," each could benefit by the diversity of strengths available. "If only my brother were as good as I am at details" would be replaced with "I'm glad he's so good with the larger picture because I get fascinated with—and sometimes stuck in—the details." Instead of being critical about how others aren't prioritizing their lives and aren't spending their time, energy, talents, money, and other resources "correctly," each family member would be eager to know how they might help the others and how the others could help them. Curiosity would replace criticism. Bartering would replace berating.

Imagine the powerful effect when each person feels valued for his or her contribution to the whole. One wife grieved, "If Bill would just acknowledge my equal contribution to our home and family, it would make all the difference in how I feel about us, and it would actually make me want to give even more."

Imagine the strength available if each family member was able to see himself as an indispensable part of a whole—a "united we stand, divided we fall" whole. Moroni understood the importance of a united effort and attributed the downfall of his troops to the division that sapped his army of its strength and vigor: "We could have withstood our enemies that they could have gained no power over us. Yea, had it not been for *the war which broke out among ourselves;* . . . if we had *united our strength* as we hitherto have done; . . . we should have dispersed our enemies" (Alma 60:15–16; italics added). Truly, unity is strength.

Let's talk more specifically about working together as a family and as friends. What helps? What hinders? Most of us grew up reading the story of the Little Red Hen and feeling sorry for this hard-working chick, while being disgusted with all her friends who let her down when it came to making bread.

But again, there's always more to the story. Perhaps the friends of the Little Red Hen would have a different story to tell about the pain and pleasures of working with poultry.

"Little Red Hen? Oh, she's a great gal but she always needs things done her way, so I learned long ago just to let her do it alone."

"She gets so cranky. Every ingredient has to be put in just

perfectly. I used to enjoy making bread with her, but she took all the fun out of it with her angry outbursts."

"Actually, I always help her but she never remembers. You'd never know from the story she tells that I'm always there. She forgets what I've been doing behind the scenes to take care of everything else in her life so that she is able to make the bread."

"Little Red Hen doesn't appreciate that making bread is not what I have time to do. She doesn't seem to understand that with all the pressures in my life—family, church, business—I'd rather buy a loaf of bread at the store and spend the little free time I have talking with her instead of making bread with her."

"She's always had more energy than the rest of us. I gave up a long time ago trying to do everything she does. I just can't. Somehow I can't get this across to her and she continues to ask, 'Who will help me?' When will she understand that I'm out of gas and just don't have the energy to help?"

What would people say about working with us? Is there a little of the Little Red Hen in us? Or do we more closely resemble some another barnyard animal? Are we "sheepish" about bringing our contributions to the table? Do we "bull" our way in, not respecting others' points of view? Do we "hog" the spotlight and keep others from focusing on the task at hand by drawing attention to ourselves and our latest personal crisis? Are we too "chicken" to truthfully give our views on the project? Do we distract from the work at hand by "horsing" around?

When we successfully work together as a family or as friends, we work in a manner that brings forth the best in others and in ourselves.

Are you ready for one more quiz? Try this one.

Who is giving more?

a) Barbara, whose aging mother now lives with her, or

b) Roger, Barbara's brother, who lives in a different state but visits twice a year and sends money monthly for their mother's expenses?

This is a trick question. The answer is "both" and "neither" because the correct answer is actually "their mother, Sarah." Sarah is the most giving because her illness is bringing out the best in each of her children while bringing them closer together than they have been in years.

Prior to their mother's increased need for assistance, Barbara and Roger hadn't spoken much to each other for several years because of a competition that started between them as children and boiled up into an "anything you can do, I can do better" situation. The result was that both siblings had purchased homes they couldn't afford and were suffering in what seemed to be dead-end marriages. Barbara and Roger had something else in common: they each had a "love-impaired heart" due to years of selfish, myopic, never-think-about-the-consequences-or-about-others lifestyle. Consequently, each had a drastically reduced capacity to give or to receive love.

However, when Barbara and Roger's mother was diagnosed with Alzheimer's disease, things began to change. Sarah's illness helped her children wake up to the foolish and far-reaching effects of their long-standing feud. In their common need to provide for their mother, the siblings started to talk and forgive and reach out to each other. Each began to make changes in his or her priorities—not just philosophically, but practically—about where they would spend their time, energy, money, and other resources. There also seemed to be a parallel change taking place with Sarah and with her son and daughter. As Sarah's reality changed due to the changes in her brain, Barbara's and Roger's realities began to change due to the changes in their hearts. Sarah's children began to see one another as a great resource, a source of strength and comfort, someone to work with instead of fight against. What a gift Sarah and her illness gave to her children!

From "how to give" to "how to grieve," a troublemaking belief is: "He (or she) should do it the way that I do it." One reason the death of a child is so difficult for parents to bear is that each believes the other should grieve the way they are grieving. When their daughter Donna died, Sam and Gail were devastated but clung to each other and to their spiritual beliefs. However, after a month of turning to each other and to the Lord, Sam started to stay late at the office, schedule business appointments on weekends, and basically immerse himself in everything except his home and family.

Gail said, "Sam doesn't even seem to care that our daughter died. He won't talk about her. He wants me to remove everything from her bedroom and turn it into an office for him. It's as though he wants to forget she ever lived. I feel I'm the only one who wants to keep Donna's memory alive."

Sam said, "Gail won't move on with life. She sits around and looks at pictures of our daughter all day. She won't go out with her friends anymore. I don't think that's healthy. We know that Donna is alive and well and living on the other side of the veil. I miss her and find myself weeping uncontrollably sometimes when I'm by myself, either driving in the car or when I'm in the shower. But Gail and I and our other children are still living on this side, so I figure we'd better keep doing what we're supposed to be doing, just like we believe Donna is. I think one of the best ways we can keep our daughter's memory alive is to live our lives to the fullest, and that's what I plan to do."

Things improved between Sam and Gail only after they came to understand that each was missing Donna and grieving her death, each in his or her own way. Working to respect the other's approach, they began looking for ways to overlap their lives a bit more. From time to time Sam took an interest in the pictures Gail enjoyed looking at, and Gail started to meet Sam for lunch on days that he was going to be working late.

After they stopped turning away from each other, they agreed on one thing: grieving takes energy. In fact, it often left them exhausted. In an effort to support each other, neither got impatient when one or the other would say, "I'd love to do something with you tonight (or this weekend) but I'm just too tired." No guilt. No whining. Only understanding and comfort were offered. Sam and Gail discovered that when they both gave all that they had left—their widow's mite of energy—to each other, there really was "enough and to spare," and their marriage actually blossomed through the dark days of sorrow.

EXPERIMENT UPON THE WORD

How can the wisdom in Mark 12:44—"she . . . cast in all that she had"—strengthen your relationships? Consider the various questions and situations below and find one that allows you to think about "giving" in little different way than you have before.

a) What if there were a measuring device that calculated how much we give in proportion to the time, talents, energy, and other resources with which the Lord has blessed us? How would you show up on this Giving Scale, which could be called either the Proportion of Capacity Measurement or the Widow's Mite Meter? Would you be pleased with your rating? Would you wish it were higher? What could you do to increase your rating? What do you think would happen if you increased your "Proportion" to "Capacity" rating by even just 10%—a tithe's portion?

b) If you were fined one dollar for every judgmental thought about another's contribution or participation, which of the following activities would cost you the most money (i.e., where are you most likely to judge others' contributions or participation?):

at home
at church
at work
at a family reunion
at my high school reunion
in the neighborhood
at a women's conference
somewhere else

Monitor your judgmental thoughts for one week. Fine yourself a dollar for every pejorative thought about another that you have, particularly those thoughts related to how much they "give" to you or to someone else. At the end of the week, take the money and purchase a gift for someone on your "judgmental-thoughts-about-giving-and-living hit list."

c) Think of someone in your family who you feel is doing

less than his or her fair share. What have you previously told yourself about that person and his or her contributions?

Now, if you put the Widow's Mite Meter on this person and the meter shows that he is giving *all* he has to give—based on his *present* capacities, liabilities, and challenges—and in fact is actually giving proportionally much *more* than you, how would that affect your thoughts and feelings about this individual? How would it change your behavior toward this family member?

One man wrote: "When I think about the Widow's Mite Meter I feel chastened because of my previous opinion of my brother. I had been judging him and his contributions to our family as a 'thing of naught.' I now realize that based on our different capacities, he actually gives MORE than I give. I had not considered the demands of his profession, his financial situation, and the limited time he has available. I'd judged him wrongly—and of course, unrighteously. After looking at things from his perspective, with an eye to what he is really capable of giving, I was so embarrassed about how I'd behaved. Truly, I had been 'lifted up in the pride of [my] own eyes' (Alma 1:32), and that kept me from seeing the situation clearly. I had even persuaded myself that I am a better man than he is. No wonder our relationship had been so strained. No wonder he has always seemed so uncomfortable to be with me."

Now, think once again about that person you feel is giving less than his or her fair share. If you were to discover, and really believe, that he is giving ALL he can give, ALL that he is presently capable of giving, what would you want to do differently?

d) Consider three people in your life. Think of their strengths and weaknesses. What do they do better than you?

What can you do better than they? Now, imagine you and these three people associated in a great bartering business. How could you help them? How could they help you? In what ways could you strengthen each other? Is it possible you could provide a missing piece in their lives and vice versa? What could the four of you accomplish together that you wouldn't even consider trying on your own? How would the lives of your friends or family members be enriched if you took this approach? How would your life be improved? Does thinking about this celebration of collaborative strengths change your feelings toward anyone?

e) Consider someone you have thought of as a burden in your life. Perhaps it's someone who has seemed at times to be a bottomless pit—insatiably lapping up all you had to give to them and demanding more. Now think about Sarah and her children from the example. Do you remember that it was Sarah who was actually giving the most? Is it possible that what has seemed like a relationship where you are the lone giver might actually be the opposite—a situation where *you* are a recipient? What gift have you overlooked or been blind to? What has the person to whom you've been giving, given to you? You may just want to thank them for their gift. Watch what happens to your relationship and to your heart when you do. Because there really is more to giving than meets the eye.

CHAPTER 6

DON'T DISCOUNT YOUR PERCEPTIONS

As for myself, to me he doth not stink. —Alma 19:5

Just because others see a situation differently than we do, we shouldn't be swayed too quickly to shift our position. Peer pressure can lead us astray—even after our teenage years. We are particularly vulnerable to the opinions of those we love and admire. However, even those we highly esteem may not always see things as they really are, which is all the more reason for us to increase our ability to receive personal revelation. When we are living, and praying, to have the Spirit as our guide and then feel uncomfortable with a certain plan of action, or something "just feels wrong," we need to follow our feelings instead of following the crowd.

We need to have the courage of the little boy in the story "The Emperor's New Clothes." We need to be willing to cry out, "The Emperor is naked," even if all around us are singing choruses of "Love the robe, Emperor!" and "Emperor, the robe is you!" As we seek to build relationships of strength and trust with our loved ones, we need to be wise stewards of the promptings of the Holy Spirit, if we are to enjoy His constant companionship.

The wife of King Lamoni was wise. After King Lamoni "lay as if he were dead for . . . two days and two nights" (Alma 18:43), many were telling Lamoni's wife that he should be buried. They said his body was decaying and reeked (see Alma 19:5). His wife, however, had a different perception and sought the counsel of a prophet to confirm her impression. She said to Ammon, "I would that ye should go in and see my husband, . . . as for myself, to me he doth not stink" (Alma 19:5) She sought validation of her experience by seeking counsel from a prophet.

What prevents many of us from trusting our feelings? What constrains us from speaking clearly about our perceptions and essentially saying to those who think otherwise, "as for myself, to me he doth not stink"? Typically, we worry that we will look silly or even stupid, that someone will get upset, that we'll be rejected by people we want to like us, or we may even worry that they will think *we* don't like *them*.

We need to challenge these fears and be more like King Lamoni's wife. We need to courageously seek a confirmation of our perceptions by comparing them to the counsel of prophets and other true messengers including, and most importantly, THE messenger of the Lord, the Holy Ghost. We need to be much more concerned about offending the Spirit after He has prompted us than about offending others.

One of the fastest ways to ruin a relationship is to ignore our feelings after they have been confirmed by the Spirit.

Why? When we betray feelings that have been validated by the Spirit, we diminish our full participation in our relationship with another. On the other hand, one of the best ways to strengthen a relationship is to learn to trust the promptings of the Spirit and to speak and act in ways that are congruent with our feelings. By doing so, we establish an honest environment in which we are true to ourselves and where our friend or loved one has an increased opportunity to be more nearly who he or she really is.

Examples

Linda was a single parent who tried to fill her home with conversations and activities that would invite the Spirit. Her four children loved her and she adored them. Teachers at church and at school gave rave reviews of each child to Linda and told her she was lucky to have such obedient children. However, Linda began to feel increasingly troubled about her eldest son, 16-year-old Patrick. Although he was always willing to help, lately she felt there was something different about Patrick's demeanor. Linda wanted to respect his privacy, yet she feared that the time he spent on his computer at night was getting him into trouble. She asked Patrick outright if he were visiting pornographic Web sites. He was outraged. "I would never do anything like that!" he declared, stomping off to his room.

Linda wanted desperately to believe her son, but more and more things about Patrick added to her concern, including a change in his countenance. "He looks so dark to me. Patrick has always been a handsome young man, but lately he almost looks ugly. There's something going on with him, but he swears he's not viewing Internet pornography," Linda said to a friend.

This conversation with her friend was a turning point for Linda because the more she insisted "as for myself, to me he *doth* stink," the *stronger* her concerns became. This was not a conversation that calmed her feelings. This conversation made it clear to Linda that by *not acting* on her feelings, she was essentially denying that she had received promptings from the Spirit—promptings that were telling her Patrick needed help.

Linda's suspicions and concerns led her to obtain some software that traces Web sites visited by the computer user. One day while Patrick was at school, with some coaching from her brother who was a computer whiz, Linda installed the software on her son's computer. And then she waited.

The software delivered as promised and within a week Linda had more evidence than she ever thought she might find. All the sleazy Web sites her son was visiting and revisiting, at all times of the day and night, were tracked. She had the evidence. Now, what should she do? She told her bishop of what she'd done and what she had found. The bishop lovingly called the mother and son in for an interview—separately, and together. Patrick lied his way through the interviews, not knowing that his mother had printed out a list of all the pornographic sites that had become increasingly irresistible to him.

Later that night Linda told Patrick that she and the bishop knew that Patrick had fallen under the influence of pornography. "You can't know that, because I haven't!" Patrick yelled. Then Linda told Patrick how they knew and that she had a list of the numerous pornographic sites he had visited in the previous week.

Patrick could not believe what his mother had done and

was initially outraged. "You've trespassed my personal property and privacy! How could you do that?" he shouted.

"Because I love you. I'm your mother and I'm worried about you and I want to help you," Linda calmly replied. Picturing the Spirit being right there by her side gave her strength to speak from her heart.

It took a couple of days for Patrick to calm down, but when the bishop called him for another visit, Patrick went quite willingly. "I was ashamed and scared to tell the truth," Patrick told the bishop this time. "I could feel the pornography starting to rule my life, but I didn't know what to do about it, and I thought everyone would hate me if they knew."

Working with his bishop and a competent therapist, Patrick started on the road to recovery from his addiction. The relationship between mother and son strengthened. Linda's admiration for her son grew as she witnessed him tackling his pornography problem head on and coming clean about other mistakes and blatant sins in his life. Patrick's respect for his mother grew because of her relentless determination not to let him betray his true self. He was forever grateful to and proud of his mother for becoming a super-sleuth on the Internet and busting him.

✐

Prompted by concern over their mother's failing health, four adult children commenced talking about their mother and father one evening, and about what they could do to help their parents during this stressful time. Unfortunately, the conversation quickly turned only to talking about their dad and how nonsupportive he had been of their mother. One after another, each sibling provided yet one more detailed memory that confirmed what a tyrant their father had been and was. It was a "pick a little, talk a little, pick a little, talk a little, cheep, cheep, cheep, talk a lot, pick a little more" kind of conversation—right out of *The Music Man*. As the negative characterizations of their father multiplied, Debbie, the middle daughter, found herself feeling more and more restless. Despite all her father's failings—which she openly acknowledged—in her heart she felt about her father, just as King Lamoni's wife did about her husband: "as for myself, to me he doth not stink."

What could she do? She didn't want to be seen as "Daddy's little darlin'," nor as an ostrich that was afraid to see what had really been happening all these years, yet she couldn't deny the promptings she was having to shift the conversation. She gently interjected a question. A pretty courageous question: "What do you think Dad would do if Mom were to become even more ill and die?" Initially, her siblings continued their diatribe, but then, imperceptibly at first, each sibling started to say something rather positive about their father. Benign comments about him spending more time with them and their families merged into comments about his cooking— "Remember that chili he used to make?"—which segued into memories of their father making pancakes on Saturdays, teaching them to ride their bikes, opening bank accounts with them, and paying them $1 for every A grade they received in school. On and on, the story of a father who was involved with, and cared deeply about, his children unfolded. Quite a different story from the one that had been told earlier in the evening.

Because of Debbie's willingness to be true to her deep feelings about her father, namely, "as for myself, to me he doth not stink," her siblings were able to view their father in a positive light. This turned out to be a very timely upward shifting of their sights, because just three weeks later—and very unexpectedly—their mother did die. On the foundation of their benevolent conversation about their father, the siblings commenced building a new relationship with him, one that celebrated his strengths and that enabled them to be loving, compassionate, and forgiving toward him.

Experiment upon the Word

Let's get personal, as we apply the wisdom of "as for myself, to me he doth not stink" (Alma 19:5) to your life.

Think of a relationship in which you often hold back your true feelings. What are some of the things you fear will happen if you were to speak your true feelings? You may want to write your fears down on paper—the more fears you identify, the better.

Now, ask yourself: "How many of the things that I fear *will happen* if I speak my true feelings *are already happening*, as I conceal those feelings?" In many cases you will find you have nothing new to fear. Your fears about what *might* happen—to you, to the other person, or to your relationship—may actually be happening now *while* you are being disloyal to your true feelings.

Think of a recent conversation with a loved one that troubled you. Try to capture the essence of what each of you said. You may want to write the dialogue down. It's often useful to see the stark reality of our words in black and white. Notice those places where you betrayed yourself.

Next, write the conversation the way you wish it had unfolded, if you had actually spoken your true feelings. What is the most important thing you wish you had said? At what point in the conversation do you wish you had said it?

When one man rewrote a conversation between his wife and himself, he discovered that the most important thing he wished he had said to his wife was: "I want to work *with* you, not alone. I don't want you to say, 'Whatever you want to do is fine with me.' I want a real companionship with you. I want us to be a team."

This husband was surprised at what his rewritten conversation revealed. He read to his wife the rewritten conversation he wished they'd had, complete with his heartfelt desire to work *with* her, to form a real companionship and be a team player *with* her. His wife was delighted and overcome with emotion. Her husband's clearly expressed, heartfelt desires were an answer to her own recent pleadings with the Lord.

Make it a practice to tune into your feelings. Ask yourself the following questions.

First take a quick check: Is there anything that could be distorting your perceptions, things such as unrepented sin, medications, intense emotions, fatigue, physical impairments, or chemical or nutritional imbalances?

What do your senses—your spiritual senses, your physical senses, and your "common sense"—tell you about a particular situation or person?

How do your perceptions fit with the counsel of prophets? When you consider the words of the prophets, are your perceptions in line with what they say?

If, after considering the counsel of prophets, you are increasingly drawn to your perceptions and conclusions, appropriately declare your feelings or concerns with confidence, clarity, and kindness. Be willing to say, either in words or in your actions, "as for myself, to me he doth not stink," when all about you are preparing the coffin.

A special note for parents and others who love children: If you are seeking the guidance of the Spirit and living to hear His promptings, learn to trust your "instincts," particularly when it comes to parenting concerns. When everyone else says such things as "There's nothing wrong with your son (nephew, cousin, granddaughter's fiancé)" or "He's just going through a stage, he'll grow out of it" and yet you feel that there *is* something wrong, trust your feelings and follow through—whether it's a concern about something physical, emotional, spiritual, mental, or social.

If something smells "rotten in Denmark," it's time to relentlessly search until you find the source. Tune in and speak up even when all around you are commenting on a sweet aroma, while you are perceiving just the opposite and wanting to say, "as for myself, to me he *doth* stink." If you need to strengthen your voice, call in the cavalry. Arm yourself with the Spirit, perhaps another family member, an ecclesiastical leader, or a friend—or all of the above and more!

For the sake of the children, please don't discount your perceptions!

CHAPTER 7

Don't Look Back
at the Sordid Past

Escape for thy life; look not behind thee. —Genesis 19:17

"K eep your eye on the ball," whispers the golf coach, encouraging the player to maintain her focus solely on the goal, which is to hit the ball in precisely the right way to get a hole in one. Well, maybe someday.

In the book of Genesis, Lot's goal was to escape the sordidness of Sodom and that city's imminent destruction in order to move forward with his life. The Lord's injunction to ensure Lot's success was "look not behind thee" (Genesis 19:17).

If our goal is to move forward in our relationships, we need to follow the wisdom of the Lord's words and *"look not behind [us]."* Because the truth is that the direction we're looking determines where we're heading. We need to look forward, if we want to go forward.

As in the example of Lot and his family, however, there is

a temptation to look back at the enticements of the past. At times there almost seems to be a stronger-than-gravitational pull in that direction. These enticements may be those which we've faced personally, or they may be temptations with which friends and family members have struggled. However, when we are serious about moving ahead in our lives and creating healthier, happier relationships, we would be wise to "look not behind [us]." It's time to quit craning our necks to look back at the sordid past, and it may even be time to throw away the rearview mirror.

"But just a minute," you may say. "Isn't it *ever* useful to look back?" Of course. We honor our pioneer heritage every July 24th and mentally make the trek west with them, perhaps revisiting and reverencing the ruts made by the wheels of their wagons and handcarts. When we talk about getting stuck in the ruts of the past, the ruts over Rocky Ridge are certainly *not* the ruts of which we speak! Some ruts of the past can give us courage and strength to carry on, move on.

Looking back can be useful, if it gives us a new perspective. The angel who delivered a wake-up call to Alma the Younger urged him to look back, to "remember the captivity of thy fathers . . . ; and remember how great things [the Lord] has done for them; for they were in bondage, and he has delivered them" (Mosiah 27:16). In this case, looking back gave Alma a glimpse into the power of God, being entirely unaware, at that moment, of the blinding view he would soon be shown. With the assistance of a fresh perspective, our response, when looking back on a difficult past may be, "I've never thought about it quite that way before."

Sometimes there is hidden treasure in the past—even in a "sordid" past. While the Lord told Lot *not to look back* to

Sodom, the Lord told the sons of Lehi *to go back* to Jerusalem—a city that was also awaiting destruction because of the wickedness and unbelief of the people. Sounds like a similar scenario ("sin-ario"?) to Lot's city, doesn't it? So why such different commands from the Lord: "Look not behind thee," to Lot, versus "return to Jerusalem," to the sons of Lehi?

One difference may be explained by comparing what existed in the two cities. In Sodom there was just more corruption. In Jerusalem, along with the corruption, were the brass plates, rich with Lehi's family history and the revelations of the Lord. Similarly in our personal lives and relationship, there may be times when looking back on a sordid past allows us to retrieve previously unknown treasured qualities and capabilities about ourselves or our loved ones. For example, a woman with a tortured past of sexual abuse came to realize, by looking back, just how hardy and resilient she was to have survived such horrors (see Feinauer, Callahan, and Hilton, "Hardiness as a Moderator," 65–78). By retrieving the good qualities from her difficult past, she realized that she wasn't a "victim"—a label that had held her captive for most of her life. Instead, she realized how courageous and strong she had been and was. The word *hero* seemed to capture who she really was—a woman who had survived a travesty and was now able to help others. For the first time in her life, she felt ready to build relationships of love and trust with others, and it all started by returning to her tragic past and finding a treasured history of herself that she had never known existed.

However, when the Lord tells us that He is not going to remember our sordid past anymore—in fact, He is going to obliterate it so that there is no tragic past to remember—we need to "look not behind us." Just as the Lord destroyed all the corruption that was Sodom, with His atoning power He can wipe out all the sin and degradation from our lives and from the lives of our loved ones. The city of Sodom is gone. Our sins, missteps, mistakes, misdeeds, and inadequacies can be gone.

For many of us, the annihilation of a sordid past may seem just too good to be true. Whether influenced by disbelief or utter amazement, we may act as though we are looking straight ahead but we keep peeking in our rearview mirrors from time to time, just to check. "Could it really be true that all my bad choices and shameful behavior are really gone?" we may ask ourselves. And just as the peeking of children into the oven to see if the cookies are finished baking curtails the baking, our peeking into our pasts after we've thoroughly repented usually inhibits the very process we're trying to check on.

Just as every peek into the oven dispels some heat and slows the baking of the dough, every peek into the past—after we have confessed to those we need to, after we have made restitution, after we've sincerely started down a new and better path—slows our progress because it shifts our focus, dispels our energy, thoughts, and desires, if only momentarily.

The irony is that we can never find out if our past is gone by looking back into the past. We can only determine its absence by looking straight ahead, moving ahead, and discovering how we are different in our thoughts, feelings, and actions.

The scriptures tell us that Lot's wife disobeyed God's command and looked back. This act of disobedience, of *looking* back, was actually a *turning* back, a turning back to her old life. So it is with us. The phrase "And when thou art converted" (Luke 22:32) comes to mind. If we look back too soon after turning away from the past, our *looking* back can actually *turn* us back to our old sins. Similarly, looking back at our loved ones' sordid pasts can often turn them back to their old sins. In looking back, we risk returning to the very things of which we have repented and from which the Savior has cleansed us with His atoning blood. No wonder those who have repented are encouraged to "look not behind thee," even to the point of removing former associates from their lives (see Kimball, *Miracle of Forgiveness*, 77) and not spending time rehearsing their past sins to others.

EXAMPLES

Caroline had been excommunicated from the Church for adultery. She recognized the gravity of her sin and was truly sorrowful and eager to repent and demonstrate a sincere desire to change her ways. She walked through the rigorous process with her bishop, but unfortunately her husband, Ted, was not fully engaged in the process with her. Several years went by during which all the marital conflicts that had existed prior to the adultery continued to occur. Rather than join forces and tackle their problems together, the couple drifted into a lethal pattern of "looking back." Looking back, Ted couldn't get beyond the betrayal of his wife and continued to blame her infidelity for all their problems. Caroline also looked back—with increasing longing—to the seeming "freedom" of her adulterous days. The result? Caroline committed adultery again, evidencing the truth that *where you're looking is where you're heading*.

⁂

Bob was a single man who had never married and who struggled with an addiction to pornography. He knew his addiction prevented the Spirit from being with him and had distorted his relationships with women. Bob finally confessed to his bishop, received priesthood blessings, stopped the Internet service to his home, and did everything he could—including seeking professional help—to get out from under the grip of this ugly, relentless ruler of his life. One day a friend asked Bob how he had managed to be so successful in escaping the pornography that had held him captive. What would he tell other men who were being held prisoner by pornography? "You have to be desperate for change" was Bob's reply. Bob's desperation had led him through the gut-wrenching and heart-changing process of repentance.

Then one day Bob took an inventory of his life and concluded that although he felt so much better without pornography in his life, although it was so wonderful not to have the old, relentless buzzing in his head, although he was finding joy and guidance in the scriptures as he never had before, although he felt as though he had important work to do in his profession and in the Church—and was doing it—he was still single, and he felt all alone. He hated that feeling, and so "just for a moment" (one of those notorious moments right out of the story of Pandora's box), Bob looked back.

He peeked into his past. He entertained again the sordid pictures in his mind. And he was quickly recaptured by the seamy images—images that he had previously described to a friend as "dung" that had filled his mind, heart, and home. "Dung" that he had been so relieved to be completely rid of. Now those same dung-laden images had once again invaded and taken possession of his mind and soul.

Bob was more discouraged than he'd ever been. He felt he was the man described in Luke, who having put his hand to the

plow to make a brand new furrow, a new path for his life, now—
tragically—had looked back (see Luke 9:62). Self-loathing,
hopelessness, and despair multiplied. And of course the more
hopeless Bob felt, the more vulnerable he became to the sordid
practices of the past.

EXPERIMENT UPON THE WORD

Let's experiment upon the word by considering the places
in your life where you would be well advised to "look not
behind thee."

Start by imagining what a difference it would make to you
if the Lord were to counsel you directly, as He did Lot. What
changes would you make in your behavior if the Lord were to
give you a fresh start and instruct you never to look back?

In the first example above, Caroline and Ted realized they
had things to do, individually and together, before they could
ever follow through on the injunction to "look not behind
thee." For them, one very important step was to make a list of
the "weapons of war" they had used against each other in their
relationship. If you believe that this step is needed in your life
before you can move ahead, please see chapter 4: Bury Your
Weapons of War.

After acknowledging the weapons they had used, Caroline
and Ted still found it difficult not to look back at the pain they
had inflicted on each other. The temptation to rehash prior
offenses was so great that they even joked about what a blessing it would be if each of them had a severe and permanent
case of amnesia with regard to their past failings, foibles, and
frustrations.

Imagine what might happen if you developed amnesia and
could not remember any horrible, disappointing thing that you

or a loved one had done or endured? Where would you spend your time and energy as a person *without* a troublesome past? How would your behavior change toward yourself and toward others? What would be different?

Do you have a relationship that you believe could benefit from a case of selective amnesia? Ask yourself: "If I woke up tomorrow and had amnesia about all the disappointments I have experienced with this other person—what would I naturally be inclined to do for, or say to, him or her?

As beneficial as a case of amnesia might be for your relationships, the power of the Atonement is so much better. Infinitely better. And the results are everlasting. In a revelation on the principle of repentance, the Lord said, "Behold, he who has repented of his sins, the same is forgiven, and I, the Lord, remember them no more" (D&C 58:43). What a wonderful promise. Consider how different your life history might read if the Master Editor, Jesus Christ, were to expunge all the mistakes you have made and all the transgressions you have committed. Think about a formerly troublesome period in your life and write it the way you believe it is now written, or can be written, because you have—or will—coauthor your life with the Savior. That is the ultimate reauthoring of your life!

We've explored what happened with Caroline and Ted, but what about Bob in the second example? Well, Bob discovered that "Look not behind thee" means "Keep looking ahead." On the advice of a friend, Bob generated a list of goals he wanted to accomplish in the next 100 days, in every area of his life—spiritual, physical, financial, professional, and so on. Do-able goals. Measurable goals. These goals helped him stay focused on looking ahead.

Bob found there was something unexpectedly exciting

about the concept of 100 days. What *could* he really accomplish in 100 days? What could he do in 100 days to serve and lift others—to give as he'd never given before? What could he do in 100 days to move closer to filling the measure of his creation? What could he do in 100 days to grow closer to the Lord than he'd ever been?

Bob reviewed *daily*, not just monthly, what he had written. He memorized his goals so that he could recite them almost as a mantra to resist any pull from the past and keep his focus straight ahead.

Ask yourself, "What will I accomplish in my next 100 days because of the power that is available to me as I draw closer to the Savior than I ever have before?" Then write down the impressions that come. Review your goals at least once a week and watch what can happen in your life. In addition to maintaining your focus on the future, setting goals provides the opportunity to write your diary in advance. Complete the following as you would like it to read one year from today: "This has been the most wonderful year. I was able to accomplish . . . I was able to experience . . . !" Try it. You'll like it.

As we make goals for ourselves, the overarching-undergirding goal is to do what the Lord wants us to do. So make your list. Check it twice. Then remember that your goals are written on paper, not chiseled in stone, so be open to additional inspiration as the Lord prompts you to make course corrections by revising the goals you may have written. As you act on these impressions, you may be astonished at the pace He will move you forward.

To maintain his forward movement, Bob found it necessary to throw away his "rearview mirror." He replaced the temptation to return to the old enticements with a dogged determination to look forward—to put on a neck brace, so to speak, so that there could be no rubber necking, no turning his head to look back.

Throwing away his rearview mirror meant making even more changes in his life than he had made before. Bob put every aspect of his life under a microscope, frequently asking himself: "Does this (activity, thought, feeling, etc.) help me focus on moving forward toward a new future, or does this, in any way, invite me to return to my previous dark ways?" He revamped his environment, social network, use of free time, the music he listened to, the spending of discretionary funds, and so forth. He created a new lifestyle that supported, in every way possible, his new life—his new life in Christ.

Consider the effect it might have on your outlook and in your relationships if you were to throw away your rearview mirror. What if you were to take the energy you expend agonizing over past mistakes and invest it instead in shaping a new life, one that is in harmony with gospel principles and leads you back to Christ? Apply the wisdom in D&C 67:14: "Let not your minds turn back."

Focusing on a sordid past or entertaining memories of previous immoral or sinful behavior is in fact to "set at naught" or denigrate the power of the Atonement, which Mormon condemns as "a gross error" and "solemn mockery" (Moroni 8:6, 9). His warning is clear to those who deny the mercies of Christ and the power of His redemption: "Wo unto such, for they are in danger of death, hell, and an endless torment. I speak it boldly; God hath commanded me" (Moroni 8:21).

Examine your own life. Does your behavior consistently reflect your belief in the Atonement of Jesus Christ and His power to redeem us from our sins? If not, what changes do you need to make?

Ask yourself from time to time: "If I were living as though the Atonement were fully operative in my life and in the life of the other person, how would I handle this situation?" How would your relationships change if you were to really believe in, and seek to access, the power that is in the Atonement?

We affirm our belief in the Atonement by not looking back. We strengthen our relationships by following the Lord's injunction to "look not behind thee." And where should we be looking? Paul tells us. We should be "looking unto Jesus the author and finisher of our faith" (Hebrews 12:2).

CHAPTER 8

REMEMBER, THE CHILDREN ARE WATCHING

And after this manner of language had my mother complained against my father. —1 Nephi 5:3

Nephi noticed. He noticed his mother, Sariah, complain against his father, Lehi. He even remembered the words she said: "She . . . had complained against my father, telling him that he was a visionary man; saying: Behold thou hast led us forth from the land of our inheritance, and my sons are no more, and we perish in the wilderness" (1 Nephi 5:2). He also noticed his father's efforts to comfort his mother (see 1 Nephi 5:4–6). Later Nephi observed the effect that his older brothers' rebellious behavior had on the health of his parents:

"My parents being stricken in years, and having suffered much grief because of their children, they were brought down, yea, even upon their sickbeds. Because of their grief and much sorrow, and the iniquity of my brethren, they were brought near even to be carried out of this time to meet their God" (1 Nephi 18:17–18).

He also noticed the effect his mother's distress had on his younger brothers' feelings: "And Jacob and Joseph also, being young, having need of much nourishment, were grieved because of the afflictions of their mother" (1 Nephi 18:19).

Nephi watched the behavior of family members, observed the effects of that behavior, and noticed the feelings of all involved. That's what children do. They are exquisitely sensitive to what is happening with and between family members. For example, children notice how their parents treat each other and how their parents are feeling. Parents may be able to hide a lot of things from their children, things such as Easter eggs and Christmas presents, but it's almost impossible for parents to hide their actions and emotions. It's as though children, some more than others, are equipped with special devices to track their parents' behavior and emotions. So, if one day you're not quite sure how you're feeling, perhaps you should ask your child!

What *are* your children noticing these days? What are they picking up on? What do you observe in their behavior that might indicate how they are being affected by your family dynamics? Some children respond by mimicking what they see. If a daughter watches her father explode in anger, while observing that her mother punishes through steely silence, the daughter may vacillate between angry outbursts and muteness when problems arise. If you knew that your child's behavior is almost certain to mirror your own, is there something you would want to stop doing immediately? What behaviors would you want to increase?

Other children respond to what they notice by trying to

help. When a three-year-old suddenly starts needing more cuddling, is he really trying to comfort his parent who is sad and needs more nurturing? When a 13-year-old begins skipping school and doing poorly on homework assignments, could it be an attempt to unite her parents and stop them from fighting out of their concern for her? Could it be that a son who is misbehaving outrageously is actually being altruistic—offering to sacrifice his reputation with his parents in order to help them resolve their own conflicts? If you thought your children's behavior—good or bad—was influenced by what they notice in the family, what would you want to do differently?

Actions, however, are not the only issue. If a son sees his father and mother cheerfully working together as they pay their bills on time, grow a garden, and clean and maintain their home, he will likely do the same when he has his own family. On the other hand, if a son sees his parents arguing over the bills, quarreling over growing a garden, and fighting about the cleanliness and upkeep of the house, the likelihood that he will embrace these responsible activities is not as great.

Imagine the difference for a son when he hears his father announce in a positive tone of voice: "Your mom and I are going outside to have some fun in the garden," versus "I *have* to go work in the garden with your mother," said resentfully. Or think of the difference in a daughter's perception when she hears her mother say in an upbeat manner, "Your dad and I want to get a lot of things done around the house today," versus "Your dad is *finally* willing to help with a few things around here today," announced in a tone of exasperation. Behavior is only part of the equation. Emotions seal the deal.

What responsible behaviors are you trying to teach your children? What are your emotions related to those activities?

Remember that your children are watching both your behavior and your attitude.

Dinah and Ralph, a couple in their 50s, wanted to make some positive changes in their relationship. The wakeup call came when Dinah was diagnosed with erratically fluctuating high blood pressure. Her physician suggested that she look closely at her life and eliminate any unnecessary stress factors that might be playing havoc with her health. Dinah didn't have to look very far before she came face to face with a major stressor in her life—her marriage. It had been years since she and Ralph had really talked and taken more than a passing interest in each other. They had spent their 30 years of marriage living parallel lives, in which their activities, interests, and dreams rarely overlapped.

Over the previous 10 years, Dinah had tried to tell herself that she was okay with the situation, but now, with all the children launched from the nest, the lack of a close emotional connection with Ralph was a stark reality that was not going unnoticed by Dinah's cells and soul. So, Dinah broke the rule of silence in their marriage and described to Ralph her loneliness and her desire to spend more time with him. Though Ralph was initially caught off guard by Dinah's distress, he responded with greater understanding than Dinah had anticipated. They started to talk and to walk together. They started having breakfast together in the morning and praying together at night—two practices that had somehow been neglected over the years.

One evening, about a month later, Dinah was talking with

one of her married daughters. The conversation revealed some important insights.

Daughter: "Mom, you look so healthy and happy these days."

Mother: "I feel better than I have in years."

Daughter: "I've noticed something different about you these past few weeks. What's different?"

Mother: "Well, several things really, but I would say the biggest difference is that your Dad and I are closer than we've been in years. We're talking and laughing and doing things together. It's so great. We always kept it a secret from you kids, but I can tell you now that your dad and I haven't always been happy in our marriage. In fact, sometimes we've been quite unhappy."

Daughter: "Sometimes? Mom, I would say you and Dad have been quite miserable most of the time. I've have always known that. This isn't a surprise to me."

Mother (very surprised): "How could you have known?"

Daughter: "I have eyes, Mom. It always used to bug me how condescending Dad was toward you. He bossed you around and controlled everything you did. I watched you shrink more and more as I grew up. It was like you were afraid of him. I can remember feeling so sad for you, and so mad at Dad. But, as with most things in our family, I just kept it to myself."

This interchange with her daughter shocked Dinah. She was stunned to think that her children had always known of the marital discord. All these years she and Ralph believed they had kept their unhappiness a secret. They had been so careful never to argue in front of the children. Yet somehow their discomfort with each other had leaked out. The real secret had been that their lack of marital intimacy was *not* a secret!

The children had been watching all the time, and what had been going on couldn't be concealed from them. They had noticed what was *not* present between their parents. They were aware of the lack of connection and joy between their parents. The absence of warmth that had characterized their parents' relationship had been a powerful presence in their home!

Consistent with their new approach to their marriage, Dinah talked with Ralph about what their children had seen, felt, and known all these years. For a time the couple mused together, without blaming one another, about how they wished they had handled things differently while the children were growing up. Then their conversation shifted as they talked about the changes they were making now, and they celebrated the differences the children would continue to see.

"Dad's watching a video that he's not supposed to watch. It's the kind you tell him not to look at," sobbed Max, age 12, to his mother, as he headed for bed. Betty was in despair. Just a few days before, her eldest daughter, 15-year-old Kim, had yelled at her father on her way out the door: "If you're so worried about me doing well in school, let me tell you what keeps me from concentrating. It's not boys. It's not drugs. It's worrying about you, Dad, and what you're doing on the Internet!" Neither Betty nor her husband had seen that one coming.

How many times is this going to happen? Betty wondered. Was she supposed to just sit by and watch while her children watched their father look at base images on the television and computer? She remembered her husband's promise of a few months before: "I'll be careful," he had said, adding a rationalization, "There's nothing wrong with what I watch. I agree that I wouldn't want the kids to watch it, but I'm an adult, and this helps me unwind at the end of a day. So I'm going to watch *what* I want to watch, *when* I want to watch it—but I'll be careful *where* I watch it, and I won't watch where the children can see."

Now Betty was faced with the grim reality that it is impossible to "be careful" when it comes to pornography. It surfaces every time and blinds those who are caught in its grip to what others can readily see—both of the pornography, and of the darkness that the pornography creates in its captive puppet. Just last week Betty learned that her children had stumbled upon her husband's "viewing habits" while doing the most innocent tasks. Cleaning out their dad's truck, they had discovered a pornographic magazine hidden under the driver's seat, and while looking for stationery in their dad's office, they had found a stash of adult videos in his filing cabinet. This week, Kim had spoken aloud her fears about her father's Internet behavior, and now, here was Max crying himself to sleep because of his father's choice of videotapes.

Betty had heard enough about what the children had seen. The voices of her children aroused her maternal need to protect them from harm. She felt a surge of intense determination to stop the insanity of sitting patiently and lovingly by while her husband viewed images that offended the Spirit and wounded the spirits of her children—not to mention the spirits of her husband and herself. The jig was up! Betty knew she had to put a stop to it.

EXPERIMENT UPON THE WORD

Consider again Nephi's description of what he had observed going on between his parents: "And after this manner of language had my mother complained against my father" (1 Nephi 5:3). What "manner of language" are your children noticing in your family? Reflect on the past week as you consider the following questions:

If you are married, what did your children learn about love and marriage by what they observed in the way you relate to your spouse?

What did they learn about the art of compromising and mutual concern through watching you and your spouse?

What did they learn about the sacrifice, integrity, honesty, and responsibility that it takes to make a marriage succeed?

What did they learn about the joy and happiness that results when spouses love each other and share the details of their lives?

Now, let's focus on just one day—today—for this next question:

If today were the only chance your children would ever have to learn about how a husband and wife converse, show love to each other, forgive each other, and solve problems together, what would they learn from observing you and your spouse?

How do you suppose your children would answer the following questions, based on what they observe in your home:

What do your mom and dad enjoy doing together?

What makes each of your parents happy? What makes each of them sad?

What does each of your parents believe is the most important thing in life?

What does your mom need from your dad and your dad need from your mom these days?

After observing your parents, what have you come to believe about love and marriage?

And finally, consider how your children would respond if someone were to ask them, "If you could change anything in the way your parents treat each other, what would it be?"

Such questions call attention to what your children learn as they observe you and your spouse (if you are married); however, your conversations and interactions with your own parents, your other children, siblings, friends, and in-laws are just as influential. What *are* your children learning? What are they noticing?

Remember, the children are watching.

CHAPTER 9

CONSIDER WHAT OTHERS CAN SEE

What beholdest thou? —1 Nephi 11:14

When Nephi asked the Spirit of the Lord to help him understand the interpretation of the whiteness and beauty of the tree of life, he was told to "look." What he saw included the village of Nazareth and "a virgin . . . [who] was exceedingly fair and white" (1 Nephi 11:12–13). At that point, the Spirit of the Lord departed. The heavens opened and an angel appeared. The very first thing the angel said to Nephi was, "What beholdest thou?" (1 Nephi 11:14). That seemingly simple question can strengthen our relationships. How?

Consider for a moment that the angel may not have been as interested in *what* Nephi saw, as in what Nephi was *able* to see. "What beholdest thou?" may have meant, "What are you *presently able to* behold?" And why might that have been of interest to the angel? Because what Nephi was *able* to see could indicate, among other things, the current state of his spiritual growth and development.

A television advertisement for vision correction surgery shows a man and woman sitting on a park bench.

"That's a turtle over there," he says.

"I don't think so," the woman replies, "It's a Frisbee."

"No, that's a turtle," retorts the man. Then seeming to brag, he adds, "I've had vision correction surgery."

"So have I," the woman says calmly. "It's a Frisbee."

A few moments later, when the Frisbee hits the man, it is clear that his surgery was not as successful as he had thought.

Due to his faulty vision, the man looked at the Frisbee and saw a turtle. "We do not see what we do not see and what we do not see does not exist" (Maturana and Varela, *Tree of Knowledge*, 242).

A young man named Brian read aloud the story of Little Red Riding Hood to his university classmates. It was a great introduction to a presentation he was making. He definitely caught the attention of the class with the story, but in a way he never intended. Every time Brian came to the words "Little Red Riding Hood," he read them as "Little Red *Rodding* Hood." His classmates were confused, and at the end of his reading they asked him why he had pronounced "Riding" as "Rodding." Brian was puzzled at their confusion until he was helped to see, for the first time in his life, that Little Red's name was *Riding*, not Rodding, Hood. He had looked at the words but had never seen them the way others saw them until that moment. "We do not see *that* we do not see" (Maturana and Varela, *Tree of Knowledge*, 19).

What beholdest thou? What we are able to see is influenced

by our spiritual, physical, emotional, mental, and social growth and development. Impairments in any one of these areas affect our vision and our behavior. When we truly come to understand this idea, our hearts become less set upon trying to convince another of how "correctly" *we* see things, and more attuned to understanding the other person's view of things. We want to find out about their *present* spiritual, physical, emotional, mental, and social state so that we can offer our ideas, our love, our concern, and our affection in ways that will make sense to them. And one of the best glimpses into another's state of being is afforded by finding out what the other person is able to see or to hear by asking, "What beholdest thou?"

EXAMPLE

Tom and Nathan are two brothers who had been in chronic conflict with each other since the death of their mother three years prior. With both of their parents now deceased, they disagreed about what should happen to the family home and many other issues regarding their parents' estate. During the previous three years each brother had spent countless hours trying to convince the other of the error of his thinking. And when they were apart, the brothers spent just as many hours planning what to say when they were together.

Managing the estate was becoming an obsession with each brother. Tom's wife often found him working late in his home office as he poured over facts and figures. "I've got to figure it out once and for all so that it's an 'open and shut' case. Then Nathan will have to agree with my way of thinking," Tom would say to his wife. She would roll her eyes and go back to bed knowing that she would soon be facing another day as a "single parent." "It doesn't feel like I even have a husband," she protested. "I feel like I'm on my own trying to raise our kids and manage the house while Tom figures out one more game plan about that dumb estate."

Nathan's wife and children noticed a dramatic decline in Nathan's health. He was eating and sleeping poorly, gaining weight, and becoming more and more lethargic and apathetic about every other area of his life. Nathan's wife was very concerned. "We've got to put an end to this conflict," she said. "It's going to kill my husband if it continues much longer. Secretly I wish the family home would burn down and all the estate money be given to charity. I made the mistake of saying something like that to Nathan one day. He got so mad at me and said that I didn't understand. I guess I don't."

The conflict and feuding continued until one day when a friend said something to Tom that enabled him to change his view of Nathan, which had been that Nathan was "pigheaded," "stubborn," and "stupid." The new idea allowed Tom to change his entire way of looking at the whole estate mess.

"Think of it this way," the friend said. "You and Nathan each have biological or physical parts, and you each have a psychological, social, and spiritual makeup. In short, you are biopsychosocial-spiritual beings." At first Tom was a bit overwhelmed by the cumbersome term, so he divided the word into segments to help him understand how it related to Nathan. *Bio*, for biological and physical, referred to Nathan's physical being—a part that was becoming very unhealthy. The *psycho*, or psychological aspect, was the part of Nathan that Tom believed was pretty messed up. As he thought of Nathan's *social* part, Tom had an immediate flashback to several childhood memories when Tom felt badly for Nathan because he didn't have any friends. And Nathan's *spiritual* part? Tom hadn't ever thought about that. What *was* happening to his brother's spirit, and to his brother's relationship with the Lord, in the midst of all the conflict between the two of them?

Tom's friend helped him understand that each and every aspect of a person's biopsychosocial-spiritual being influences how that person sees something and, therefore, how they respond. The internal state of a person, *not* the external stimulus, determines how someone will respond to a situation. The friend explained that Tom could not *make* Nathan change his mind by simply presenting stronger and stronger arguments because it is a biological impossibility to *make* someone believe something.

Tom thought of the words to the hymn, "Know This, That Every Soul Is Free," and the truth expressed there about how the Lord influences us:

> He'll call, persuade, direct aright,
> And bless with wisdom, love, and light.
> In nameless ways be good and kind,
> But never force the human mind.
>
> (*Hymns,* no. 240)

Tom realized that he had been trying to *force* Nathan's mind. With the help of his friend, Tom became more and more aware that Nathan's current biopsychosocial-spiritual state was what dictated what his brother saw and how his brother responded.

Tom wondered if Nathan's biopsychosocial-spiritual state could ever change and permit Nathan to be open to Tom's ideas.

"Absolutely," his friend confirmed. "Actually, Nathan, like all of us, is changing all the time. Every encounter with the world, with others, and with you influences his cells and his soul. Nathan can change. He can even change his mind. He may even change his mind about the estate. But I can almost guarantee you that it won't happen if you keep trying to force your ideas on him as you have for the past three years. It's like someone once said: 'A man convinced against his will is of the same opinion still.' That isn't just a nice psychological premise, it has been shown to have biological roots."

Tom recalled the Simon and Garfunkel song that says, "A man hears what he wants to hear and disregards the rest." That's how he usually felt about Nathan. "He only hears what he wants and totally blows me off," Tom complained to his friend. The friend explained, "I'm sure it seems that way, but let's go back to the idea about how a person's present 'structure or state' determines what they see or hear. With this in mind, we would actually change the words of that song to be: 'A man hears what he is presently *able to* hear and disregards the rest.' Nathan hears what he is able to hear—based on his present biopsychosocial-spiritual structure—and he disregards the rest, because it doesn't fit—meaning it doesn't fit with his structure *at this particular time*. Your reasoning and conclusions literally don't show up on his radar screen."

This new way of looking at things had a dramatic effect on Tom. He began to understand that Nathan's cells and his soul would need an opportunity to change *before* he would be able to hear and see things differently. Then, as Nathan's biopsychosocial-spiritual state changed, he could be more open to ideas he hadn't considered before. Some things that did not "fit" for Nathan right now might be a "fit" for him later.

Tom also began to recognize that Nathan was not trying to be defiant and ornery and that perhaps Nathan's inability to see things Tom's way had actually been magnified by the way Tom had forced Nathan to listen to his ideas, how he negated all Nathan's ideas, and how he belittled Nathan in the process. None of their prior confrontations had done anything to create an environment where Nathan's cells and soul could grow and develop.

Tom was able to see Nathan in a different light—as a brother instead of an adversary whom he had to dominate and convince. Tom lost his urge to work out one more argue-proof plan. Instead, he felt drawn to understand Nathan. If Tom was going to offer ideas that might be a better "fit" for Nathan, Tom needed a better understanding of Nathan's "present state."

Tom had been so focused on the disposition of the estate and on being right that he had not considered his brother's state at all. What *was* happening with Nathan—physically, psychologically, socially, spiritually? That question prompted Tom to start phoning Nathan more often to talk about things other than the estate—sports, kids, Nathan's work, Tom's work, life in general. Initially, Nathan seemed hesitant to talk with Tom, perhaps thinking that his brother's newfound interest in him was just another of Tom's schemes to get his own way. But Tom's sincerity eventually convinced Nathan to relax, let down his guard, and make an investment of his own in their friendship.

It caught Tom off guard that with his new understanding, he actually felt freer to be even clearer about his point of view regarding the estate. His freedom increased as he *offered* his ideas to Nathan instead of *forced*, as he *invited* instead of *demanded*, as he *opened* instead of *pushed*. Nathan's positive response to Tom's respectful, genuinely interested, and yet still clear position is evident in the following e-mail that Tom sent to his friend:

"Just one more thing. I called Nathan on Sunday. Out of the clear blue, I felt like I needed to connect with him and follow up on having a family meeting. We talked for about twenty minutes, and I felt like I stood strong in my opinion about still meeting with an attorney. He doesn't want to, and I told him that was okay but that I still had some questions that I needed to have answered so I would just meet with the attorney by myself. I told Nathan that I felt like it was important that we take a look at things and make sure everything is handled the way Mom and Dad wanted them handled. I felt really good after talking with him."

Tom and Nathan's family estate is still in the process of being settled. What is more important is that two brothers' hearts are healing, and their wives and children feel as though their husbands and fathers have come home from their war against each other.

EXPERIMENT UPON THE WORD

Think of one of your relationships that needs help and apply the following:

"What beholdest thou?" when you think about that relationship after reading this chapter? What do you notice about yourself, about the other person, and about the relationship that you may not have noticed before?

Now, take a moment and think about the notion that each person has a biopsychosocial-spiritual structure—a structure that is highly malleable, yet a structure nonetheless—that *determines what* each person is presently able to perceive and, reciprocally, is *influenced by* what each person beholds.

First think about your own structure. Impairments or underdevelopment of any aspect of that structure—biological, psychological, social, or spiritual—can constrain what you are able to see around you and restrain how you are able to respond. For example, firmly held beliefs can prevent us from seeing what we're looking at. Think of Mary grieving at the garden tomb. Because of her sorrow and her belief that the Savior was dead, she initially did not *see* Him even though she *looked* at Him (see John 20:15–16). Similarly, the two disciples on the way to Emmaus looked at the resurrected Christ and walked and talked with Him, "But their eyes were holden, or covered, that they could not know him" (JST, Luke 24:15).

What might be obscuring your vision these days? Is something keeping you from seeing what is right in front of you? Perhaps you are prevented from truly seeing because of a constraining idea about yourself or about a loved one or about life itself.

Now think about your loved one. How do your thoughts and feelings about your loved one change when you seek to understand that person's *present* biopsychosocial-spiritual structure? What is there in their past experience, environment, physical condition, mind-set, or receptivity to the Spirit that is influencing what they *are able to see* and, therefore, how they respond? Do you notice that your efforts to consider *what* your loved one can see and what is influencing this decreases your inclination to blame or find fault with them? What do you notice?

Now, think of a recent difficulty in your relationship. It could be any impasse, but let's say that you and your teenage daughter have been locked in a dispute over how late she may stay out on the weekends. You both have strong views and have reached a stalemate that has put a real strain on your relationship. How different would your response be if you let your daughter know that you are genuinely interested in understanding what she is presently able to see as she looks at the situation? More specifically, "What beholdest thou?" could translate into:

How does she view the situation and you?

What kinds of limits make sense to her?

What would be a reasonable compromise from her point of view?

You can use this approach to resolve any number of conflicts in any relationship. Try it and see what happens.

Examine the way you interact with your loved one. Have you unwittingly begun offering your ideas and assistance in ways that fail to respect their present state or their ability to choose what fits them individually? Notice the ways you might have unintentionally done this.

Find ways to stop *forcing* and start *offering*; to stop *demanding* and start *inviting*; to stop *"pushing* people through doors," as one young man stated, and instead start *"opening* doors for people." Invite your loved one to reflect on your ideas and the help you offer, so they don't feel forced or pushed or shoved, and so they can choose what *presently* fits them.

Consider the following example of what can happen when we *invite* others to reflect on our ideas, rather than trying to "force-feed" them:

Joanne had taken a huge step when she disclosed some very personal things to one of her friends. Her friend was truly interested in Joanne and after hearing the situation, offered her some friendly advice. But there was no assumption that Joanne would accept the counsel or any demand that she should change in any way. There was only genuine interest expressed and an invitation made to consider another point of view. Joanne felt no pressure and remained free to accept or reject what had been offered.

Rather than instructing Joanne what to do, her friend had simply asked "What beholdest thou?" or in other words, "Based on our conversation, what are you able to see? After all we've talked about, what fits for you at this time?" Joanne wisely added to the decision-making process, prayer—the quintessential oasis of reflection and a powerhouse of new perspective. Here is Joanne's e-mail response to her friend:

"I'm not sure how to tell you this, but something happened to me today. It's like my eyes were opened, my prayers were answered, and my heart softened. I have been so mad at you! I felt you just weren't listening to me, and more than that, I believed you didn't even care. I felt like I have ripped my heart apart, trying to tell you how I feel, over and over and over again because you didn't seem to hear what I was saying. I was trusting you as I have no one else, *ever,* with tender feelings and risky thoughts, and you didn't even seem to give me a response.

"I believed you had given up on me, and I *knew* you were going to tell me you didn't want to be my friend anymore. I could feel it, even though you wouldn't ever say it. I decided I was going to quit talking to you. I have also been so mad at *me* because I drive people away from me—people who are really helping me, serving me, loving me. I have done this for years to my husband, to others, and now to you. I have prayed so hard to know what to do next. Where to go from here? I have been on my knees more in the past few days than ever before. But I have been SO MAD!!! SO SCARED!!! Today for some reason I began reading the list you suggested I make after the last time we talked. I had entitled it: 'Ideas That Are Most Helpful to Me These Days.'

"Today, when I read over that list, I saw things that I have never seen before. I knew exactly what you had been trying to say. I knew that you *had* heard me all along, and I now realize that I am the one who hasn't been listening. I re-read the e-mail I wrote to you last week, along with your response. Today I saw it entirely differently. I felt your support all the way through the e-mail.

"I was going to wait until Thursday when we are getting together, but I'm so afraid I will forget this feeling that I have right now, and I just need you to know that I'm going to be different from now on. (Please remind me of this!) I just want to commit to you right now—before something happens to the way I feel—that I *am* going to be different.

"I'm noticing things about Joe [her husband] that I haven't seen before. He has been so good to me this past week. I love him with all of my heart, and I am going to do a lot of things different with him as well."

"What beholdest thou?" What a power-packed question we can use to strengthen our relationships.

CHAPTER 10

IMAGINE HEARING
HEALING WORDS

*I say unto you, can you imagine to yourselves
that ye hear the voice of the Lord, saying unto you,
in that day: Come unto me ye blessed?* —Alma 5:16

"Can you imagine to yourselves that ye hear"? What marvelous words of invitation! There is power in imagining. Through the power of our imaginations, we can *see, hear, taste, smell,* and *feel* the "reality" of a past or even future situation. Research has shown that a basketball player can actually improve his game by sequestering himself in a room, vividly imagining himself executing certain plays or movements or techniques. Skilled golfers routinely envision the shot they wish to make before actually attempting it. When you imagine something, your cells and your spirit respond to it as though it has actually happened. Imagination is a powerful thing.

So too are words. They lodge in our hearts. Is it a coincidence that *hear* is four-fifths of the word *heart*? Could it be that as the eyes are the windows to the soul, the ear provides access to the heart? In any case, words have a significant effect upon our cells and upon our souls. Some even believe that the walls of our homes are affected by the words that are spoken within.

Words spoken by someone we love or someone in a position of authority can be both compelling and propelling. A young woman, Mary, overheard her father say to her mother in a heated argument, "Our marriage was just fine until Mary was born. She's the cause of all our problems!" Those words lodged deep in Mary's heart, distorting her view of herself, crippling her emotionally, and causing her to forever doubt her ability to be loved or bring joy to others.

A man, successful in his profession and relationships, recalls that when he was a teenager, a coach he idolized once said to him, "You're good enough to play professional baseball." Though he ultimately decided not to follow that dream and later in life suspected the coach's assessment had actually been unrealistic, that off-handed remark created a feeling of confidence in the young man that remained with him and not only made him a better baseball player than he would have been, but also gave him the confidence to achieve other things in his life.

Sometimes words spoken by someone we hardly know, or may not even really like, can have an equally powerful effect. After speaking in church, a young man was approached by an older man. The young man had never met the older man, who proceeded to give the young speaker some pretty tough, unsolicited feedback on his talk. Although the feedback was negative, the outcome was positive. From that moment on, the young man changed how he prepared himself to teach. Words can change not only our thoughts and feelings—they can change our behavior (see Cook, *Teaching by the Spirit*).

Now consider the enormous impact it might have if we combine the power of imagination with the power of the spoken word: "Can you imagine to yourself" the power that you can access when you imagine hearing certain words being spoken to you?

In Alma 5, we find multiple invitations from Alma to evaluate and improve our lives. In Alma 5:16, he invites us to imagine ourselves in the ultimate situation—hearing the voice of the Lord call us by name and say, "Come unto me ye blessed, for behold, your works have been the works of righteousness upon the face of the earth."

For many, imagining the Lord saying these words to them may seem impossible. Knowing our weaknesses and imperfections, we may be able to imagine hearing the Lord say those words to *others*, but never to *us*. And, in a similar way, it is impossible for many of us to imagine hearing a family member or friend say words that would heal our hearts and enliven our relationships. Yet those are the very words we long to hear—words such as: "I knew you had it in you," "I'm here to apologize to you," or "Thank you for all you do to bless my life."

EXAMPLES

Sandra was distressed about her life. She was unhealthily overweight and felt trapped in turbulent relationships with her husband, son, and daughter. Oh, how she wished things were different! Where was that magic wand when she needed it? Then one day she stumbled onto what would help her most. "I need to hear something I've never heard before—something that would make all the difference. I wish I could hear my mother say, 'You were a good daughter.'" But her mother had died on Sandra's wedding day, 25 years earlier.

Sandra started to think about her childhood, concentrating on memories of her mother. She imagined being in her mother's presence. She could see her mother, picture where they might be sitting together, and what her mother would look like. She could picture her mother's hands and, most importantly, she could hear her voice.

For Sandra, the question-stem posed by Alma, "Can you imagine to yourself that ye hear the voice of . . . ?" was completed with "your mother saying unto you, 'You were a good daughter.'" And the answer to the question was "Yes." Yes, Sandra *could* imagine it! And imagining it summoned feelings from the depths of her soul—feelings that had lain dormant for 25 years but were now bubbling up in a torrent. She found herself sobbing uncontrollably for several minutes. Healing tears flowed as she felt the truth of what she had imagined hearing her mother say: "Sandra, you were a good daughter. A very good daughter."

Although she had "only" imagined it, this experience felt incredibly real to Sandra. "Actually," she said, "it felt like one of the most real things in my life. I'd felt so numb for so many years that I couldn't remember the last time I felt as alive as I did then. For years, whenever I tried to listen to people, I felt as though I was submerged under water. I could hear them speaking, but their voices were muffled, and I couldn't really tell what they were saying. But when I imagined hearing my mother say those words, I heard her voice so clearly. And somehow I feel different. It's hard to explain, but imagining hearing my mother say, 'You were a good daughter,' freed my heart to experience life and to love again. It sounds kind of corny to say, but that's what it feels like to me."

Sandra reflected often on this experience, imagining over and over again her mother's healing, lifting, liberating words, "Sandra, you were a good daughter." Day after day. Week after week. And the truth of those words took hold and triggered several positive steps forward in Sandra's life and relationships.

Sandra experienced an increased desire to remember her mother in other ways. She pulled out old family photographs that had been buried in the basement for years and introduced her children to their grandmother, really for the very first time. She found some audiotape recordings of her mother. Hearing her mother's voice on audiotape intensified the reality of the imagined experience. One day Sandra called an aunt with whom she had only had limited contact for many years. She couldn't believe how much her aunt's voice sounded like her mother's. She had never noticed that before. So, along with receiving an update on her extended family members, Sandra received the gift of once again "hearing" her mother's voice as she spoke with her aunt.

Validated by her mother's approval, Sandra noticed that as the weeks unfolded, her own mothering improved, as did her enjoyment of being a wife. She really *was* free to give and receive love in a way she had never been before. When it came to love, what had always felt like a risk to her before, now felt like a privilege. It was an honor to connect with those she loved, an opportunity to bring to her family all the love she remembered receiving as a child from her own mother.

Sandra also discovered that her need to stuff herself with food was diminishing without her usual struggle to control her eating. She came to realize that much of her unhealthy eating

had been an unconscious attempt to soothe the painful feelings that she had disappointed her mother and that she had
not been a good daughter. Now, however, immersed in the
truth of hearing her mother say, "You were a good daughter,"
Sandra felt free to be all she could be—a great woman, wife,
and mother.

✎❥

George was concerned about how he was replicating his
father's angry outbursts. "I'm doing the very same thing to my
wife and children as my dad did to Mom and us kids. I swore
I'd never be like him, and here I am—a carbon copy! I just
hate myself for the pain I'm causing my family, because I
remember that same pain from my own childhood."

When a friend asked if it would make a difference if
George could hear his father apologize, George immediately
protested: "Oh, I can't imagine my father ever apologizing. I
don't even think my dad knows the words, 'I'm sorry.' He just
wouldn't ever do it. That's way too far-fetched!"

In an effort to help George begin to imagine this longed-
for but seemingly impossible scenario, the friend suggested that
George try to visualize his father through the lens of a video
camera hidden in his father's home. "Just imagine this,
George," his friend said. "It's 2:00 A.M. and you see your father
pacing the floor." George could picture the room his father
would be in, complete with details of colors, furniture, and
lighting.

The friend continued, "You know this is real because
you've hidden the video camera, and are watching your father
'live.' Your father is crying and saying out loud, 'I'm so sorry

that I was so cruel to my son. I'm so distressed about the horrible names I called him when he would break something or do something wrong in his effort to help me on our farm. Why did I tell him that he was worthless and would never amount to anything? He was only a boy. He was learning. I was his father and should have mentored him instead of beating on him with my violent temper. George is such a great man and was always a fine son. I wish I could let him know that I've always seen his goodness. Perhaps I was intimidated by the greatness of his spirit.'"

After replaying several versions of this imaginary scenario, George visibly relaxed. Tears flowed as he "listened to" his father's voice, saying those things he so longed to hear.

For one month George spent a few minutes each morning replaying in his mind the "videotape" of his father's confession, hearing and seeing the apology and basking in the words of commendation. He felt different. The message was penetrating his mind and finding a place in his heart. At the end of the month George reported that his angry outbursts had ceased almost entirely. He found himself able to express love and appreciation to his wife and children, and he was even looking forward to a visit to his father's home to help him with some farm work. Imagining what he longed to hear had commenced the healing of George's heart—healing that had eluded him for decades and had wreaked such havoc in his relationships.

EXPERIMENT UPON THE WORD

Take a few quiet moments to accept Alma's invitation to "imagine to yourself that you hear" words that will heal your heart and enliven your relationships. You may want to write down your reflections and date them. It's quite possible that even a few weeks from now your answers will be different. Remember that change really is possible when we imagine to ourselves that we hear certain words—even seemingly "impossible" words.

Start by thinking about the effect it would have on you if you were to hear the Lord call you by name and say: "Come unto me ye blessed, for behold, your works have been the works of righteousness upon the face of the earth" (Alma 5:16). Just for a moment, put all your protests aside that that could never happen and answer the following questions:

What would you feel even more urgency to do with your life?

What tendencies, habits, attitudes, or behaviors would you want to eliminate?

In what ways would such an endorsement from the Lord change how you view your relationships or treat your loved ones?

Now, let's zero in just a bit more. What are the specific words—spoken by the Lord to you—unique to your life experiences, that could change everything—or at least many things—in your life? For example, what words from the Lord would free you to be more loving and forgiving of others? What do you long to hear from the Lord that would cause many of the problems in your life and your relationships to simply fall away?

Now let's focus on words spoken by others in your life. What are the words you long to hear from one of your friends or family that would make all the difference to your relationship and to your life? Really think about it. What specific words, spoken by whom, would make a difference to how you feel, or how you think, or how you act?

Use the words of Alma: "Can you imagine to yourselves that ye hear the voice of" (that friend or family member) "saying unto you, in that day" (the words you long to hear)?

If your answer is "Yes, I *can* imagine it," skip the next two paragraphs. If your answer is "No, I *can't* imagine my loved one ever saying those words I long to hear," ask yourself this question: What would need to happen for you to imagine—just to imagine, for even just a moment—such a seemingly impossible thing actually happening?

As you reflect on this "impossible imagining," ask yourself:

What effect would it have on me if I were not only able to imagine it, but if the person actually said those words?

What would you be able to do that you can't do now?

What would happen to your cells and your soul if you were to hear one of your loved ones say: "There's something very special about _____ (insert your name). She or he has some unique gifts and I believe she or he is going to accomplish many wonderful things"? Who is the person you most wish would say those words?

Now think about how your relationship with a friend or family member would change if you were to overhear that person say, "I really want to do such and such,"—and the thing they desired to do was the very thing you have been longing for this person to do (or not do), the very thing that would bring your spirit to life. For example, the desire might be to show you more warmth and affection; be baptized; talk with you more; be more involved with the kids; go with you on a trip; clean the garage or basement; study the scriptures with you; pay their bills; pray with you; go to the temple instead of boating; forgive you and never bring up the past again; apologize.

One husband, who felt rejected and neglected by his wife, imagined hearing her say, "I want to be closer to you. I want to spend more time with you. I long to hold you and to be held by you." Just *the prospect* of hearing those loving words from his wife infused this husband's heart with energy and joy. By rehearsing this imaginary scene several times, he found the strength to speak from his heart and take responsibility for their failing marriage in tender ways he'd never done before.

Truly, unfathomable possibilities are opened when we imagine hearing those we love speak healing, enlivening words.

CHAPTER 11

HELP OTHERS TO
LOVE ONE ANOTHER

And he [Elijah] shall turn the heart of the fathers to the children, and the heart of the children to their fathers.

—Malachi 4:6 (see also 3 Nephi 25:6; D&C 128:17–18)

Think about Elijah's altruistic mission. His was not to turn the hearts of the fathers and the children to himself. Rather, his mission was to turn the hearts of the fathers to the children, and the hearts of the children to their fathers so that ultimately, saving temple ordinances can bind one generation to the next. Elijah's work is calculated to strengthen the bonds between family members, to get them thinking about each other, loving each other, and wanting to be with each other—forever.

Perhaps we can draw inspiration to strengthen our relationships from Elijah's selfless mission and example. Instead of worrying about how many people love and appreciate *us*, we can endeavor to help others love *each other*. We can work to turn the heart of a father to his children, and the children to their father; the heart of a sister to her brother, and his to her; or the heart of a mother-in-law to her daughter-in-law, and vice versa.

Parents, regardless of their present marital status, can help turn the heart of their child to the other parent. This can be done in small and simple ways. Many widowed or divorced parents keep on display photographs of each child with each parent.

Parents who no longer live together or who have ceased to love each other will want to keep their marital strife from adversely affecting their children. An embittered spouse who speaks ill of the other parent or who turns a child into a confidante or a surrogate spouse usually causes emotional problems for that child. Though it is hard to do, one of the best ways to insulate children from the stress and conflict is to resist "bashing" the other parent and instead find ways to build him or her up in the eyes of the children. One recently estranged father, who for years had joined his daughters in complaining about their mother's insistence they all go camping, was finally able to see that particular family outing through very different eyes. One day, as his teenage daughters were once again whining about not wanting to go camping, he took the opportunity to say in a quiet, nonjudgmental, and almost nostalgic way: "Girls, we (using the plural pronoun, which indicated he was including himself) don't go camping because we love camping. We go camping because your mother loves camping—and we love your mother." In that moment, the estranged father turned the hearts of his two daughters to their mother. The daughters' hearts were also turned to their father as they listened to his expression of respect and love for their mother, something for which they had longed for years.

Consider the following questions as you think how to apply the wisdom in Malachi 4:6: "And he shall turn the heart of the fathers to the children, and the heart of the children to their fathers."

Are you selfless enough to be more concerned about turning hearts to others, rather than to yourself?

Are you confident enough in your loving relationships to do so?

Is there someone whose heart you could help turn to another?

What do you think would happen if you tried?

What message of love and concern could you take from one person to another?

Whose heart might benefit if you were to tell someone how much he or she is admired by another person?

Can your voice strengthen another's message and their voice, and in the process strengthen the bonds between the sender and the receiver?

Are you willing to be a messenger of love?

Do you wish to be a healer of hearts?

EXAMPLES

A concerned mother observed that due to the long hours he spent at work and his quiet manner when he was home, her husband's tender, loving heart was going unnoticed by their children. She was worried that her husband's love for their children, which she knew was true and deep, was a best-kept secret from the children. In the spirit of Malachi 4:6, she looked for ways to turn the hearts of the children to their father, and the heart of the father to their children.

What did she do? She became his spokesman. In everyday conversation, she would express her husband's feelings for his children. She would say things like: "Your dad is so thrilled for you and what you've been able to accomplish," "He's so proud of you," "Do you know how much like your father you are? He really likes (basketball, salmon, reading) just like you do," or "Your dad said the funniest thing the other day. It made me laugh right out loud. We were talking about . . ."

And she conveyed the most important truth: "Your daddy loves you very much."

Because he was unable to say it himself, the mother became the messenger. Without her willingness to be his voice, the children would not have known the depth of their father's love.

At the same time, the mother would say to her husband such things as: "The kids got such a kick out of that story you told me," "I overheard our son bragging to his friend about what you do at work," and "The kids think you're great. They love you so much and they love being with you."

And what did she notice? She was amazed to find that the children gradually shifted from being quiet and a bit awkward around their father to being playful with him, showing their delight to be with him, being eager to tell him about their day, and asking for his help with their homework—even if it meant they had to stay up late in order to see him (and of course staying up late seemed to be an additional perk!). The hearts of the children were being turned to her husband, their father, in very observable ways. She had been the messenger who had carried to the children the comforting assurance that their father loved them, took delight in them, and was a fun guy with great ideas. Her voice had been his voice.

All this helped her husband as well. Responding to her assurances of his children's love and affection for him, his heart was turned more warmly to them. The children became real to him, more real than they'd ever been. Instead of viewing them as something of a disruption, he began to enjoy their antics and take pleasure in the time he was able to spend with them. And the more he was with them, the stronger their love for each other grew. The heart of the father had truly been turned to his children, and the hearts of the children had been lovingly turned to their father.

Carol felt hopelessly neglected by her husband. He was so devoted to his work, she wondered if he was devoted to her at all. In fact, she wondered if she even showed up on his radar screen. Did he ever think about her? Consider her feelings? Feel a need to talk to her? She struggled, wondering what to do with her feelings of loneliness and neglect. She thought of saying something to him, but what would she say? She didn't want to be one of "those nagging, whining wives who only drive their husbands further away."

Then, one day, one of her husband's colleagues mentioned to Carol, just in passing, that her husband talked about her all the time at work. Carol was stunned by this "newsworthy news," and obviously delighted. That was all she needed to hear. It was as though her husband's colleague had been her husband's "Aaron" (see Exodus 4:16), speaking words on behalf of her husband that Carol needed to hear. And the

"Aaron effect" was dramatic. Carol's heartbreak and loneliness fell away. Her eyes and ears were opened, and she was able to notice other things that her husband did that spoke of his love for and devotion to her. Carol's heart was turned to her husband upon discovering, through the eyes and ears of an observer, that her husband's heart was in fact turned to hers.

EXPERIMENT UPON THE WORD

Before we begin to experiment with the wisdom in Malachi 4:6, "And he shall turn the heart of the fathers to the children, and the heart of the children to their fathers," let's talk about a caution: There is a difference between a *messenger* and a *meddler*.

A meddler is so invested in the outcome that he or she seeks to micromanage the relationship between other people. The meddler dictates behavior rather than offering information. For example, the meddler says, "You really should give Jim a call" or "You need to spend more time with Brittney."

On the other hand, a messenger carries messages of love and concern from one person to another, and then—out of genuine respect for the agency of each individual—allows each of them to choose what to do with the information. His or her role is to gently expose one person to the heart and mind of another, but never to dictate what either person should do.

Now, with that distinction and caution in mind, let's proceed. Are you acquainted with two individuals you love whom you believe could benefit from a closer bond? These would be persons for whom you have some responsibility—for example, two relatives, two friends, two coworkers in the Church, two neighbors, or your children and your spouse. Again, please be aware that this is risky business when it comes to adjudicating others' relationships, but if you prayerfully approach this mission of being a messenger, and your motives are pure, it's possible you'll perform a great service.

Think of yourself as a type of Cupid, a messenger of love whose righteous desire is to turn the hearts of the two individuals to each other. Now, consider the following questions:

Why would it be a blessing for these two to have a better relationship? Would it contribute to their happiness, rid them of turmoil, or improve the situation in the family, home, neighborhood, church, or workplace?

Is there anything that is self-serving in your answer to the first question? If there is, you may not be able to convey messages of love and then stand back and just watch. Chances are that before you know it, you'll soon become a meddler because you will be far too invested in the outcome.

Can you imagine a beneficial outcome, if these two people were to be reconciled or if one or both of them knew something they are not now aware of? Is there something you can do or say that will expand their understandings, warm their hearts, or take away some pain or frustration? Take a cue from Nephi when he wrote, "I would that ye should know . . ." (1 Nephi 1:18; see also 1 Nephi 7:1). His noble motive was to help people understand what his father, Lehi, had *tried* to do. What is it that you would most want your two friends or loved ones to each know about the other? What, if your friend were to hear it, would facilitate healing or take away some kind of pain or misunderstanding?

As you consider that question, keep this in mind: Some of the most comforting, welcome, and heartwarming messages a person can receive are those that validate that person. "Do you know how much Alice admires you?" "I know for a fact that

Felicia wouldn't hurt you for anything." "You and Harold have so much in common." "Erin was just saying the other day how badly she feels that the two of you have lost touch."

Such kindly messages speak directly to the heart and can lead to understanding, healing, and reconciliation.

With this in mind, what "heart turning" message might you deliver from one person to another? Prayerfully review your decision, while bearing in mind the possibility that perhaps you should not deliver any!

If you feel the Spirit directing and blessing your efforts, have the courage to convey the loving words, concerns, and expressions of admiration the Lord has put into your heart. Then let D&C 123:17 be your guide: "Cheerfully do all things that lie in [your] power; and then may [you] stand still, with the utmost assurance, to see the salvation of God, and for his arm to be revealed."

After you've done all you can, then stand still and watch how the Lord magnifies your efforts.

What a privilege it is to be a messenger of love and a healer of hearts. There is no greater or more sacred trust.

CHAPTER 12

LET YOUR LIGHT SHINE ON THOSE YOU LOVE

I give unto you to be the light of this people.
—3 Nephi 12:14

Plants and flowers flourish in the presence of light. The same is true of other growing things, such as children, friends, parents, siblings, spouses, and relationships.

We know that the Savior is the source of *all* light (see D&C 88:6–13) and that love, truth, power, and the Spirit coexist with light. The more *light* in our lives, the more *love* we feel, the more *truth* we are drawn to, the more *power* we receive—the kind of power that magnifies our influence for good—and the more often we experience the promptings of the *Spirit*.

These five elements—light, love, truth, power, and the Spirit—in any combination, operate to bless our lives. Knowing this can help us as we seek to strengthen those we love and our relationships with them. When we offer true love to others, we are also inviting more light into their lives. When we share an experience where the Spirit is present, love increases. When we offer a truth, power is included. Thus, as we bring light to others' lives, the more open to the Spirit they can be, the more love they can feel, the more truth they are able to embrace, and the more power they can access. And, gratefully, the cycle goes on and on.

When we shine our light on someone we love, that light brings love and truth and power and the Spirit to our loved one and to our relationship. No wonder the Savior said, "I give unto you to be the light of this people" (3 Nephi 12:14). It's important to note His choice of words: "be the light." He didn't say, "Be a club unto this people and beat them into submission to my truths." He didn't say, "Be a stick unto this people and whip them if they get off course." He didn't say, "Be a prod unto this people and move them where they don't want to go." The Savior said, "Be the light."

We are drawn to light. We are cheered and warmed and comforted by light. We are inspired by light. Just imagine what is possible when we bring our light, which is His Light, to others through the conversations we have and the activities we share.

Examples

Janice was desperately concerned about what was happening in her family. As a single mother of four children, ages 16, 18, 19, and 22, she was mindful of the struggle her children were having as they tried to be loyal to her and her values and lifestyle, while they were also compelled to be loyal to their father with his differing set of values and lifestyle to match.

Janice had always had a good, supportive relationship with

her children. For example, her 19-year-old son was only 15 when he cracked the code on her husband's cell phone answering service and uncovered the evidence that her husband was having an affair, something that Janice had suspected but had not been able to prove to that point. Prior to finding this evidence, her husband had continually denied his extramarital involvement, declaring that Janice was out of touch with reality and that her worries were all in her head.

Janice had been divorced now for three years and had dealt with many concerns with her children during those years. She felt that most of the concerns were normal, typical challenges of raising teenagers, but a few concerns seemed to arise from the distress of the divorce. Overall, however, Janice thought that she and her children were weathering their new, although unexpected, lives quite well.

But lately, things had changed in her home. Her children had become increasingly obstinate. They openly defied her efforts to set curfews and limits on their behavior. While just a few months before her children had enjoyed hanging out with her and bringing their friends to the family home, now they were hardly there. It especially alarmed Janice that her children's behavior increasingly reflected the undisciplined lifestyle of their father, complete with drinking, lying, and sexual involvement.

What had happened? Earlier, her children had been so willing to go with her to church, and had demonstrated great determination to keep the Word of Wisdom and to live morally clean lives. Now, they seemed to be breaking every rule in the book. It was as though she had looked away—just for a minute—and everything had dramatically changed.

Janice had to admit she *had* looked away. Although only

in her 40s, the arthritis in her hands had become increasingly painful and immobilizing. A few months before, she had begun taking a powerful new pain medication. It had a debilitating effect on her. Instead of spending the majority of her time enjoying meals, conversations, housework, and homework with her children, she was now spending her time in isolation in her upstairs bedroom. Initially she could hear the children downstairs, still happy to gather with their friends within the safety of their home. But as time wore on, she became more and more withdrawn. The medication dulled her senses and left her feeling really "out of it." It was difficult to find the energy or focus to talk to them or monitor their activities. She also grieved that she had lost her ability to discern the Spirit.

Janice's inability to feel the Spirit was a truly great loss to her. Her single parenting hadn't seemed so "single" last year because of His daily comforting guidance. But now, in stark contrast, she felt all alone and in despair. What could she do? Everything felt so dark.

As Janice prayed about her situation she felt prompted to call her physician and get off the heavy medication. She would work with him on a new approach to managing the pain. Her focus now needed to be on managing her children and main-taining her relationships with them. As her mind began to clear, she talked with a friend about her concerns. During the conversation a light went on in Janice's heart and mind. She knew what she needed to do: She needed to turn the Light back on in her home and in the hearts of her children. She needed to "be the light" to her children.

Janice realized that she had not been giving herself enough credit for the powerful influence she was in her children's lives. This realization lifted her spirits and infused her with courage.

It was time to bring her positive influence back into their lives. As she thought more about her situation, she saw that for a period of time—due to the heavy medication and the resulting prolonged time she spent in her bedroom—she had hidden her light under a bushel. During this time, her children had not had the benefit of her light, which meant that they were also out of range of her love and the truth, power, and influence of the Spirit her light used to bring to them.

Her friend tried to tell Janice that it was not her fault and that her children were personally responsible for their unwise choices, but Janice could see that her unavailability had contributed to the struggle they were having. She understood that living without *her* light for several months, and therefore living without her love, had increased her children's vulnerability to counterfeits of love. Had living without her light also meant living with less truth, which would have increased their susceptibility to lies about life and love? Had living without her light meant living with decreased power—the power to resist temptation? Had living without her light meant living with a dramatic decrease in the presence of the Spirit in their lives, which reduced the amount of Light they felt? When Janice shut herself away in her bedroom, closing the door on her children and preventing her light from shining into their lives, had the ensuing darkness contributed to the downward spiraling of their thoughts, feelings, and actions?

Thinking about these possible connections didn't make Janice feel guilty. Instead she felt Light coming back into her life as these thoughts took hold in her heart and mind. She felt powerful—more powerful than she'd felt in months. She was a mother with a mission—a mission to "be the light" to her children. It was time to bring the Spirit, love, truth, and power back into their home, hearts, and relationships. And she could do it by being a light to her children.

Janice realized that if she were going to have sufficient light to share with her children, she would need more Light *in her own* life. So that's where she started. For months she had let her scripture reading slide because it had been so difficult to concentrate through the fog of medication. She determined to once again immerse herself in the scriptures as a way of getting her own spiritual batteries recharged. Janice also added fasting back into her life, along with frequent prayers. As the mother of her home she knew she had the ability to cast darkness out and to invite the Spirit back in abundance. And she did. Relentlessly. Daily.

Janice began to attend the temple again, something that she loved doing but had neglected for the past many months. She could feel the difference temple worship made in her life. Every time she attended she felt the blessing Joseph Smith had asked the Lord to bestow on those who serve in the temple: "And we ask thee, Holy Father, that thy servants may go forth from [the temple] armed with thy power, and that thy name may be upon them, and thy glory be round about them, and thine angels have charge over them" (D&C 109:22). Janice was buoyed by His divine power, name, and glory, and sustained by angels as she returned home to nurture her family.

With more Light in her own life, Janice was ready to "be the light" to her children. Understanding the interconnection between light, love, truth, power, and the Spirit, she knew she could start anywhere. She began by apologizing. She apologized to her children for sequestering herself away and not being available to them. Their mother's apology caught the children off guard. They had anticipated anger and chastisement from her because of their misbehavior. Janice's apology invited the Spirit immediately into the conversation. Experiencing the presence of the Spirit was such a contrast for the children and such a relief that they couldn't restrain their tears, and they wept with their mother. The Light was starting to shine in their hearts and in their home again.

In the days and weeks that followed, Janice dispersed even more of her light by expressing appreciation to her children individually for something each had done or said, recently or in the past. She expressed her love to each of them and told them individually how blessed she was to be his or her mother. A feeling of *love* and the comforting presence of the *Spirit* were palpable during these moments, and one by one the children began to open up and confess their past errors. Grateful to have their mother back, they found it an easy thing to express their love for her, and as they spoke the *truth*, they discovered a greater desire and more *power* to resist former temptations. The lights were coming back on in her children's lives because their mother had chosen to "be the *light*" (not a club, not a stick, not a prod) to them. When Janice let her light shine right into their lives, they could not resist the love, truth, power, and the Spirit that accompanied it.

$$\mathscr{L}\text{❥}$$

In the midst of an extremely difficult time in their marriage, when Eric was turning away from Carolyn and from the Lord, Carolyn prayed to know what she could do to counter the gathering darkness in Eric's life. She sensed that to withdraw from him would do little good and only leave Eric more vulnerable to greater temptation. Carolyn wisely decided that the times when she most wanted to pull away from him, due to his offensive behavior, were exactly the times he needed her light the most. But how could she "be the light" to Eric when he seemed so devoted to darkness?

Although Eric refused to pray with her, Carolyn determined she could certainly continue to pray *for* him. She prayed to know *how* to pray and *what* to pray for. She prayed for the darkness to leave Eric and for some way to bring him back into the light. Then one day she discovered how she could pray *with* Eric. While she was holding him, Carolyn would cry out in her heart and mind: "Heavenly Father, please help Eric feel my love for him. Please help him feel Thy love," she would plead. Night after night as she held him, with all her might she would seek to draw upon the powers of heaven in his behalf. By day she initiated ways to spend time with him—taking a drive or going for a walk—all the while silently praying "with" him. While visiting his parents, sitting side by side on the couch with the kids, or even when he rubbed her feet late at night while watching TV, Carolyn continued to pray "with" Eric. Little did he know the light, love, truth, power, and influence of the Spirit that were being called down upon his head by his wife during those times.

In addition to praying "with" Eric, Carolyn thought of another way to expose Eric to her light. She realized that for years they hadn't really looked at each other. When *was* the last time she had looked deeply into his eyes? What color were they anyway? Well, she was going to find out, and she was going to focus her light, in laserlike fashion, right into Eric's eyes. And she did.

She began looking at him when they would converse. At

first it was only a glance. She didn't want him to be blinded by her light! But gradually she let her gaze linger a bit longer, looking first *at* his eyes, then *into* his eyes. Initially, he didn't seem to notice. Then a couple of times he reacted uncomfortably. "What are you staring at?" he would ask. But after a time he began to relax and even returned her gaze. As she would look at him, Carolyn would think, with as much sincerity and intensity as possible, "I—love—you, Eric." The words were spoken only in her mind, but the emotion was communicated through her eyes, along with extra light.

Carolyn's efforts to "be the light" paid off. It didn't happen immediately, and at times the cost/benefit ratio seemed way out of whack. Over time, however, Eric was increasingly warmed by Carolyn's *light,* and he began to remember *truths* about himself. He felt her *love* and the love of the Savior, both of which gave him the courage to embark on the arduous road to repentance. Thankfully, he was ready and felt he had the *power* to do it, thanks to the increasing influence of the *Spirit.*

EXPERIMENT UPON THE WORD

To begin this experiment, identify a loved one who needs more light in his or her life. Who is it who needs *your* light? For whom can you "be the light," and to whom can you bring the Light of the Savior? Pray to know *how* you can bring more light into his or her life.

If you are to be a source of light, you need to make sure your own wattage is high enough. Perhaps you believe that sixty watts are sufficient for your needs, but you'll need the highest wattage possible when you are trying to shed light on another.

So begin, as Janice did, by looking closely at your life.

Examine every practice—from what you watch on TV and what you read, to what you listen to and the thoughts you entertain. Do these activities illuminate or cast dark shadows? That's the litmus test.

Pursue those things that generate light and power. Pray with more feeling, fast with more purpose, study the scriptures more consistently, and participate more often in temple worship, and you'll be ready to glow!

If the person you seek to help has been immersed for some time in darkness, shedding "indirect" lighting on him or her might be the first and most useful thing to do. Indirect lighting in a room casts a glow, provides warmth and comfort, but doesn't necessarily allow you to see clearly everything in the room. If someone has been in great darkness, it may be too uncomfortable to suddenly expose him or her to full and direct light. Pray for wisdom to proceed at the appropriate speed.

Don't be discouraged. The situations they faced might have seemed overwhelming to Janice as she sought to reclaim her children and to Carolyn as she worked to save Eric from destroying himself and their marriage. But with the help and guidance of the Lord, by exercising faith and never giving up, they were each able to dispel the darkness and draw their loved ones back into the Light that illuminates the way to "peace in this world, and eternal life in the world to come" (D&C 59:23). Guided by the Light, you can "be the light unto this people"—your people. You can do it.

CHAPTER 13

HAVE HEART-TO-HEART
CONVERSATIONS

What desirest thou? —1 Nephi 11:2

In 1 Nephi 11:2, the Spirit of the Lord asked Nephi, "What desirest thou?" And what did Nephi desire? To see what Lehi, his father, had seen—namely, the Tree of Life. In answer to Nephi's desire, he was shown the Tree of Life and much more.

When the Savior asked three Nephite disciples what they desired of Him, they were afraid to say what they really wanted. But the Savior knew their hearts and must have astonished them when he declared: "Ye have desired the thing which John, my beloved, who was with me in my ministry, . . . desired of me. Therefore, more blessed are ye, for ye shall never taste of death; . . . for ye have desired that ye might bring the souls of men unto me, while the world shall stand" (3 Nephi 28:6–7, 9).

What do you *really* desire? Not just want. Not just kind of would like to have. What is your heartfelt wish? What is the deepest yearning of your soul?

If we could be like Nephi and freely express the desires of our hearts, consider how different our relationships might be. When spouses, parents, children, siblings, and friends speak from their hearts to one another, blaming and defending, criticizing and condemning, typically fall away. Misunderstandings nearly evaporate.

For example, a husband blurted out to his wife: "I hate my older brother. He was always so mean to me." Later as they talked, she listened to his heart and asked him in her own words, "What desirest thou?" Speaking from his heart, the husband said with deep feeling, "I always wanted to be like my brother. I asked for his football jersey number in high school because I looked up to him and wanted to feel close to him. I've never told anyone that before. I love my brother and I want him to love me."

If your heart could speak, what would it say? Reciprocally, if your loved one's heart could speak, what do you suppose you might understand that you haven't known before?

Perhaps you feel you already know the desires of your loved one's heart. But chances are, it may be more accurate to say that you *used to* know. Desires can change because circumstances change.

Consider the shift in thinking that was required of the Lord's people when He told them that He no longer required or desired burnt offerings. Christ instructed the Nephites, "Ye shall offer up unto me no more the shedding of blood; yea, your sacrifices and your burnt offerings shall be done away, for I will accept none of your sacrifices and your burnt offerings"

(3 Nephi 9:19). Following the crucifixion and resurrection of Christ, there was to be a new pattern of worship. Instead of burnt offerings, which were to prepare the people for the coming of the Messiah, the Lord now required of the people a new kind of sacrifice—a broken heart and a contrite spirit, which would grow out of an appreciation of Christ's atonement, the ultimate sacrifice. A burnt offering, that used to have meaning, no longer does.

Do you know what your loved one most desires *today?* One husband, David, experienced the fallout from not staying current with his wife's desires. Very early in their marriage he had to be away from home on a business trip. He missed his bride, and wanted to let her know of his love. He purchased a beautiful coat for her and brought it home, along with a note indicating that the coat was a symbol of how he wanted to wrap her in the warmth and protection of his love. His wife, Allison, was thrilled and grateful. However, 20 years later, in the midst of David's ever increasing number of business trips and protracted time away, Allison abhorred her closet full of long coats, shorts coats, dress coats, casual coats, swing coats, jackets, ponchos, and parkas. One day she pled from the depths of her heart: "I don't want any more coats. I want time with *you.* That's what would help me feel warm and protected." She no longer wanted the *symbol* of his love. She wanted to *experience* his love firsthand, by spending time together. David needed to update his understanding of the *present* desires of Allison's heart. As well, she needed to appreciate the *intent* of his.

"I know thy heart," the Lord said to Thomas B. Marsh, who was president of the Quorum of the Twelve at the time (D&C 112:11). The Lord knew that Thomas's heart was filled with love for his brethren, yet He also acknowledged "there have been some few things in thine heart and with thee with which I, the Lord, was not well pleased" (D&C 112:2).

Do you know the heart of your loved one? Are you willing to look deep into that person's heart to see the good intent and the love that is there, even if there have been a few things with which you were "not well pleased"? Think of Pahoran who, after being misjudged and censured by Captain Moroni, did not take offense. Instead, he looked on Moroni's heart, rejoiced in the greatness he found there, and chose not to be angry (see Alma 59–61).

And finally, when we've looked into our loved ones' hearts and acknowledged the goodness—even the greatness—there, and heard their answers to the question "What desirest thou?" what are we then willing to do in order to respond to our loved ones' desires? What becomes the commitment of our heart?

Consider what Abraham taught us about how the Lord works: "There is nothing that the Lord thy God shall take in his heart to do but what he will do it" (Abraham 3:17). What a comfort, to know that *anything* the Lord takes into His heart to do, He *always* does. Now, think of the comfort we could provide our loved ones, and the constancy we could bring to our relationships, if our loved ones had reason to be sure "There is nothing that [your name] shall take in his [or her] heart to do but what he [or she] will do it"!

EXAMPLES

A husband and wife were contemplating divorce. They thought they had talked about everything. Actually, they had yelled and sulked and pouted and criticized and withdrawn and fought about everything. They had hidden their true feelings behind angry outbursts and accusations. They had focused on their fears and frustrations. Then one night, out of desperation and fear, they spoke to each other from their hearts. Putting aside all their anger and frustrations, vindictiveness and vulnerabilities, they finally got to the question, "What desirest thou?" Each was able to articulate the deepest desires of his and her heart.

The wife was able to say, "I love you, and care so much about you becoming all you were meant to be. I know that I've let my childhood fears and frustrations keep you at arms' length. I'm so sorry for that. I regret the irresponsible purchases I've made. I want to support your dreams for our family, and I want to express my dreams in ways that you can hear them. I apologize for never really letting you know that I want to work *with* you and not against you in improving our lives spiritually, physically, socially, emotionally, mentally, and financially.

"Your opinion of me is more important to me than any other person's on the earth. I need to feel that you like me and would choose me all over again to be your wife. When I know that you believe in me, it makes all the difference in how I think and feel. It even boosts my energy level. I believe in us and in our mission as spouses and parents. I would love to link arms with you and get on with building a wonderful family."

The husband was finally able to say, "I love you and want to be the man, husband, and father I'm supposed to be. I've been living beneath myself far too long. In the process I haven't buoyed you up and supported *your* growth. You've had to struggle to accomplish all you have, against all odds—particularly considering your childhood—and against my thoughtless crushing of almost every one of your dreams and desires. I've been far too focused on finances. I've let money—

actually my father's obsession with money and my misdirected efforts to be loyal to him—hold my heart hostage. I know there have been times when I've given you reason to feel like I love money more than you or that I'm more devoted to my father than I am to you. I love you and want you to feel loved. I believe I've been stingy with my love, just as I've been stingy with money. I need your help to find the balance between being responsible about living within our means, and being so fixated on every dollar that we don't really 'live.'

"Your touch is what I live for. When you hold my hand, everything feels right with the world—with our world. I too believe we have a great mission to perform that requires us to work together as husband and wife. I believe that there is power in our union that we haven't yet begun to even imagine, let alone, tap into. I really want to build our marriage—a brand new marriage with you."

Each spouse continued from that day forward to be mindful of two things:

1. To speak the desires of his or her heart in a way that the other could hear.

2. To think about, and listen to, the desires of the other's heart.

Their daily heart-to-heart conversations, which many days were only ten minutes in length, were the mortar that this couple used to successfully build the marriage of their dreams.

✐

One day a daughter reflected on what she believed was a missed opportunity to speak from her heart to her father at his deathbed. In talking with a friend she regretfully said, "I wish

I'd had someone by my side to coach me so I could have said out loud the things I was feeling, but didn't dare speak for fear of crying."

What did she wish she had said? "Dad, I'm so sorry this is happening right now. We've known this "graduation" was coming, but I'm not ready to have you leave this earth. Part of me is happy for you to soon be free from the pain your body has been in. But the biggest part of me is going to miss you so much. It's scary to think of you leaving. It's such a big step. You've always known just what to say to keep me going and growing. Now I'm going to be an orphan, a 40-year-old orphan. I know that's not really true, but that's what it feels like right now. I hope you know how much I love you, and how grateful I am to have had your guidance, protection, wisdom, and love as your daughter.

"I wish I could take away the physical pain you're feeling. I hope you aren't afraid of what's ahead. Just remember all the wonderful truths we've talked about over the years about the reality of life after this mortal probation. Thank you for all you've done to give me roots and wings. You've been a marvelous father, and I will always need your fatherly assistance and advice. We've talked about how thin the veil is and about how those on the other side can reach through and assist their loved ones. Well, Dad, I'm counting on you parenting me through the veil. Say 'hi' to Mom. Tell her thanks for all she's done to help since she's been on the other side."

After verbalizing her thoughts to her friend, the daughter decided to record the words she wished she had spoken to her dying father. From time to time she reread them, once a week initially, and then once every couple of weeks. Each time she read them she imagined her father being right there by her side saying, "You didn't say those words out loud, but I knew your heart."

EXPERIMENT UPON THE WORD

Identify a relationship that could benefit from a heart-to-heart conversation. Let the scripture, "What desirest thou?" guide you through the following experiment. If possible, talk with your loved one and invite him or her to complete the experiment as well.

Answer this question: If the Spirit of the Lord were to come to you, as to Nephi, and ask, "What desirest thou?" how would you answer? If you were then granted that desire, what difference would it make in your life and in that relationship?

Now consider your loved one's heart. If the Holy Ghost were to ask that person, "What desirest thou?" what do you suppose the response would be? Really think about it. Believing that to be his or her heartfelt desire, what does that make you want to do?

Next think about, and preferably write down, the dialogue between you and your loved one that would heal or cheer *you* the most at this time. In creating the dialogue, consider the following:

The things you would like to say to clear the air, make things right, correct a misconception, make amends, describe your true feelings, or otherwise express your frustrations, fears, or concerns. Remember, there is no need to be embarrassed or hold back. The aim is to strip away all pretense and expose your heart, freely expressing your deepest desires in this relationship.

Include what you would most want to hear from your loved one. What could he or she say that will end a feud, lift your spirits, put an end to an anxiety, heal a misunderstanding, relieve your guilt, or reassure you of his or her love? You are in charge of this conversation. There is no limit to what you can imagine your friend saying.

This is worth the time it will take. Think of yourself as the scriptwriter for your heart. What does your heart long to say? What does it long to hear? Ponder. Pray. Write. Read what you've written. And then, ponder, pray and write some more.

Now write another dialogue. This time from the point of view of your friend. Script the conversation that you believe would heal or cheer *your loved one* the most at this time. Consider his or her disappointments, frustrations, fears, and longings. Put yourself in that person's place and try to imagine the words that would best serve to comfort, warm, reassure, or encourage him or her. What would your loved one welcome hearing from you?

Writing from his or her point of view, script the expressions you believe that person would most want to say to you. What is it they would ask from you? An apology? An acknowledgment of his or her feelings? Words of encouragement or forgiveness? Recognition of something noble they have done? Words of love, admiration, and commitment?

Again, take your time. Free up your imagination. Ponder. Pray. Write. Read your script. And then, ponder, pray and write some more. Seek additional insights and be open to the spiritual promptings that will come.

After writing your dialogues, put them away in a safe place. Let them cool. Pray about what you've written. Lapsed time and prayer are an eye-opening combination! Several days later go back and read what you've written. What would you change now? Delete? Add?

When you have each completed your writing, set a time when you and your loved one can be alone. Or, if you have not felt comfortable speaking about this to your loved one, adapt the following instructions as you read the dialogues by yourself.

Choose a place that you believe would feel the most safe and comfortable for each of you to read the dialogues together—the two dialogues which you have written, and hopefully, the two that she or he has written. You choose the time and place for reading what you have written; let your loved one choose the time and place for reading his or hers.

Now the written words will become spoken words, as each of you give voice to the dialogues. For example, when reading the first dialogue you have written, you should read the parts you would most want *to say* to your loved one, while your loved one reads the parts you would most want *to hear* from him or her. For the second dialogue, you read the parts you believe your loved one would most want *to hear* from you while your loved one reads the parts what you believe he or she would most want *to say* to you. Obviously you'll use the same process in reading the dialogues that your loved one has written. Caution: As you read the dialogues, read them just as they are written. Don't defend yourself. Don't explain yourself. Just thank your loved one for the opportunity to get to know her heart a little better, and for her willingness to get to know yours. Such a conversation has the potential to truly heal your hearts and restore a precious relationship.

CHAPTER 14

Don't Settle for Less

They shall return again to their own place, to enjoy that which they are willing to receive, because they were not willing to enjoy that which they might have received. —D&C 88:32

Have you heard more haunting words than these: "They shall return again to their own place, to enjoy that which they are willing to receive, because they were not willing to enjoy that which they might have received"? Unfortunately, this scripture applies to many of us who "return again to [our] own place"—to our old vicious cycles and destructive patterns of thoughts, feelings, and actions—"to enjoy that which [we] are willing to receive"—conflict, loneliness, lackluster friendships, mediocre marriages, and lifeless parent-child relationships—"because [we are] not willing to enjoy that which [we] might have received"—great friendships, marvelous marriages, and fulfilling parent-child relationships.

Let's ask some tough questions for a moment.

Are you settling for a less-than-marvelous marriage because you are not willing to invest the time and make the effort it will take to build a stronger, more fulfilling relationship with your spouse?

Are you settling for a tension-filled parent-child relationship because you're not willing to do more commending and do less controlling of your loved one?

Are you settling for a shallow friendship because you are trying to turn your friend into you rather than celebrating and enjoying the uniqueness of that individual?

Are you settling for an ongoing battle with your brother because you are not willing to forgive and apologize?

Are you settling for a distant relationship with your sister because of petty jealousies, past misunderstandings, and the pride that prevents you from reaching out in love and reconciliation?

Are you settling for a strained relationship with an in-law when a little more understanding and tolerance on your part might heal old wounds and end a fruitless power struggle?

Are you settling for an arm's-length relationship with the scriptures, one which leaves you feeling confused, much like Laman and Lemuel when they said: "We cannot understand the words which our father hath spoken" (1 Nephi 15:7) because you're not willing to focus, study, pray about, and feast on truths that can answer all the questions of your heart? Nephi's answer to his brothers, "Have ye inquired of the Lord?" (1 Nephi 15:8), gives us the key (namely, prayer) to finding answers to our problems through the scriptures.

Are you settling for a routine temple experience because you're unwilling to do what it takes to really worship there and have the mysteries of God unfolded to you line upon line, as you are endowed with power?

Are you settling for being sad and lonely because you're not willing to make the changes necessary to be happy?

Are you settling for living in a financial mess because you're not willing to live within your means and enjoy the peace that comes from paying an honest tithe, living providently, spending responsibly, and adding regularly to your savings?

Are you settling for living beneath your potential because fear, laziness, indifference, selfishness, or resentment are preventing you from bringing your best effort to the table in your family, the Church, and your chosen work?

Are you settling for just going to church on Sunday because you're not willing to do what it takes to feel your wounded spirit being healed and your load lifted as you prayerfully and purposefully partake of the sacrament? (See Ballard, "Sacramental Covenant.")

Are you settling for a deteriorating relationship with your spouse because you have sought comfort outside your marriage, in inappropriate conversations or actual illicit sexual experiences that are a betrayal of your covenants?

If you are married, are you settling for the best sex the *world* has to offer when you could be enjoying a sexual intimacy that rejuvenates your body *and* your spirit and binds you more closely not only to your spouse but to God? (See Watson, *Purity and Passion.*)

And why would we settle for less? Why would we not be "willing to enjoy that which [we] might have received"? Could it be that:

We don't believe we have the ability, talent, time, or energy to make something new happen?

We don't believe anything will ever really change?

We are being held captive by old, destructive habits, such as laziness, and continually take the path of least resistance and, therefore, the road *most* traveled?

We don't believe anyone will really care?

We don't really believe we deserve to be happier, more fulfilled, and more loved than we are?

We have grown accustomed to living beneath ourselves and beneath our privileges?

When we live beneath ourselves, we think, feel, and behave in ways that betray our true selves. When we live beneath our privileges, we don't act in ways that are consistent with the light and knowledge we've been given (see *Discourses of Brigham Young*, 32).

Isn't it time to challenge our old constraining beliefs and behaviors? Isn't it time to cease settling for a "return again to [our] own place"? In fact, isn't it time to do whatever it takes to break out of our old place? And isn't it high time to put an end to our self-destructive ways and begin claiming those blessings that are right there, waiting for us to receive them? It is. It's time for us to show that we truly believe the marvelous promise the Lord made when He said: "Ye are little children, and ye have not as yet understood how great blessings the Father hath in his own hands and prepared for you" (D&C 78:17).

One of the best ways to break out of our old, settling-for-less patterns, and to quit living beneath our privileges and ourselves, is to make sure that our view of life and love is not the world's view, but instead reflects the grand truths of the restored gospel of Jesus Christ. The world speaks from its base of knowledge. But that knowledge is limited. Describing our mortal view of things, Paul the apostle said, "For now we see through a glass, darkly" (1 Corinthians 13:12). It's true. It's the best the world can offer. But how tragic if we live and love according to the world's understanding when we could be enjoying relationships influenced by the light and knowledge the Lord has offered us.

We need to be sure that as we seek to strengthen our relationships and solve the problems that arise that we draw upon gospel truths we have access to, including truths about premortality, our relationship to God, the Fall, the Atonement, resurrection, priesthood power, saving ordinances, ongoing revelation, and eternal life.

Example

Newlyweds Carla and Dennis sat on the front row of the chapel. A fireside on marital intimacy was about to begin. Sadly, for the first 15 months of their marriage, they had been like far too many husbands and wives and had settled for an intimacy that was patterned after the sexual behavior portrayed in the world. Because they didn't know any better, they had not achieved the sacred intimacy they might have enjoyed together.

They had come to the fireside, prompted by a vague feeling of discontent in their marital relationship. Each had experienced the dull ache expressed so well in the old Peggy Lee song: "Is That All There Is?" The couple had come to the fireside, keen to learn something that would help them not "return again to their own place."

At the end of the evening neither Carla nor Dennis could move from their seats. It was as if someone had immobilized them with a stun gun. As the speaker walked by their pew on her way out of the building, Carla and Dennis reached out for her hand and asked, "Why didn't anyone ever tell us about these things before?"

Their whole perception of sexual intimacy, which had been based on the world's views, had been shaken up. Here they were, members of the "cool generation," who supposedly knew everything there was to know about sex. Yet tonight they had been introduced to concepts more powerful than anything ever portrayed on MTV. The fireside speaker had talked about achieving sexual intimacy that is "out of this world," quite precisely because it is *not* of this world!

Carla and Dennis were amazed. Neither had ever considered truths about marital intimacy such as:

Purity and passion go together (see Watson, *Purity and Passion*). What a best-kept secret! This concept was 180 degrees different from what they'd been led to believe through their exposure to movies, TV, and popular music over the years.

Purity enhances passion. Carla and Dennis had never even considered the idea that the more pure their thoughts, feelings, and actions, the more fulfilling and enjoyable their marital intimacy could be. This again was news to them. "Does everyone else know this?" they wondered.

Passion that has been purified by the Spirit ("pure passion") is always greater than impure passion. Why? Because the Holy Ghost will "increase, enlarge, expand, and purify all the natural passions and affections" (Pratt, *Key to the Science of Theology*, 61).

Pure passion enhances and is foundational to true marital intimacy. Carla and Dennis had never considered that the biggest "turn on" could be turning off the TV and turning to the Lord!

True marital intimacy is to be a soulful experience—uniting not only the bodies but the spirits of each spouse (see Holland, *Of Souls, Symbols, and Sacraments*). This was a revelation to Carla and Dennis. Every movie and video they'd ever seen focused only on physical union. The possibility that there was more to sex than that made them want to put their lives under the microscope to discover anything that might prevent them from joining their spirits—things such as anger, resentment, unwillingness to forgive, fear, and unrepented sin.

True marital intimacy is symbolic of how united marriage partners are. Carla and Dennis already knew that spending inordinate amounts of time away from each other put a stress on their marriage. But tonight they heard it in a different way. They were reminded of the importance of being together, not just in the bedroom but in every facet of their relationship. In an effort to strengthen their union, they determined to enjoy more meals together, talk more, and take walks and find other activities to share, instead of always "dividing and conquering" their days. Carla and Dennis liked this idea. Wasn't that why they had married in the first place—to spend as much time together as possible? Yet even in the first year of their marriage they had discovered how easy it was to drift into a pattern of living separate and parallel lives.

True marital intimacy is a kind of sacrament. A time for couples to renew their vows by drawing close to each other and to the Lord. Now this truth really threw them! They had never thought about sexual intimacy as a spiritual experience. And yet they were each surprised at how true that concept felt. They loved the thought that a husband and wife are never closer to the Lord than when joined in true marital intimacy.

Marital intimacy is endorsed by the Lord. Indeed, one of the earliest commandments He gave the inhabitants of this earth was, "Therefore shall a man leave his father and his mother, and shall cleave unto his wife: and they shall be one flesh" (Genesis 2:24). In their worldly view of sex, Carla and Dennis had never considered that it was a commandment from the Lord that they be intimate with each other. What they had learned was that the Lord expects married couples to invite the Spirit into every facet of their union, including their marital intimacy.

Carla and Dennis returned to their home in a very different frame of mind than they had had prior to the fireside. With the above truths about marital intimacy in their hearts and minds, they were ready to work together in letting those truths enhance their marriage. "They were [very] willing to enjoy that which they might have received."

EXPERIMENT UPON THE WORD

Think of one of your relationships that you wish were stronger. Now consider the scripture in D&C 88:32: "They shall return again to their own place, to enjoy that which they are willing to receive, because they were not willing to enjoy that which they might have received."

Ask yourself the following questions:

What have you been settling for in this relationship?

What do you believe might be possible for you and your loved one to experience or accomplish if you were to really claim all the blessings that the Lord offers you?

What have you felt a prompting to do lately that you

believe would move your relationship one step closer toward what the Lord has in store for you?

What does your partner think the two of you are missing because you've been settling for less? Talk with your loved one about what he or she believes is possible.

Now, take an even closer look at your relationship. Are your "gospel roots" showing? If you were to increase by just 10 percent the way gospel truths about life and love influence your thoughts about yourself, your loved one, and your relationship, what would you be able to do that you can't do now?

Choose one gospel truth about life or love. Write it down. Ask yourself: "If I were to act as if I really believed this gospel truth, what would I be naturally drawn to do or say?" Let that one truth thoroughly, totally, and completely influence your relationship for one week. Then the following week, choose another gospel truth and use it as the guide for your thoughts, feelings, and actions in your relationships, and watch what happens.

There really is more waiting for us to experience and enjoy with our loved ones. So much more! So don't settle for less!

CHAPTER 15

THE SEARCH THAT NEVER ENDS

He that diligently seeketh shall find; and the mysteries of God shall be unfolded unto them, by the power of the Holy Ghost . . . ; wherefore, the course of the Lord is one eternal round. —1 Nephi 10:19

Do you know the children's song:

This is the song that never ends.
It just goes on and on, my friends.
Some people started singing it
Not knowing what it was.
And they'll continue singing it forever
Just because this is the song that never ends.
It just goes on and on, my friends . . .

The wonderful truth is that when we begin searching the scriptures for the wisdom that will strengthen our personal relationships, it becomes a search "that never ends. It just goes on and on, my friends." This is so because the scriptures are multilayered. We uncover one concept or spiritual insight only to find another lying beneath it, and it becomes a search that literally never ends. Tutored by the Spirit, the deeper we delve, the more we find. We keep uncovering more. Understanding more. Discovering more.

THERE'S MORE WISDOM WAITING

When the resurrected Savior appeared to and taught the people on the American continent, He could tell they yearned to experience the same things He had offered the people in Jerusalem (see 3 Nephi 17:8). So He invited them to bring any who needed to be healed. And He healed them. The Savior also invited them to bring their little children to Him. Then, surrounded by that reverent multitude, Jesus knelt with them and offered prayer. So sublime was His prayer and so powerful were the feelings stirred in the people, they were unable to even describe what they had heard: "No tongue can speak, neither can there be written by any man, neither can the hearts of men conceive so great and marvelous things as we both saw and heard Jesus speak" (3 Nephi 17:17).

It is my testimony that when we demonstrate our willingness to heed His words and follow His teachings, the Lord delights to expand our understanding. If we are sincere in seeking it, He will send His Spirit to speak truth to our hearts and minds and open our eyes to things we have not yet even imagined.

THERE'S MORE TO IMMERSION

Too often, we read the scriptures perfunctorily—to satisfy an assignment in seminary or institute, to find a story to illustrate a talk, or to read a certain number of pages in a prescribed period of time. Though there is no harm in doing so, unless we regularly *immerse* ourselves in the scriptures, we will likely never discover the true depth of the word of God.

Immersing ourselves in the word of the Lord is not just about color coding our scriptures–although that may help. It's about adding another level of vibrancy to our relationship with the Savior.

It's not just about memorizing our favorite scriptures— although that may help. It's about letting the scriptures remind us "who [we really] are and who we have always been" (see Dew, *No Doubt about It, 35*).

It's not just about reading someone else's ideas about what certain scriptures mean—although that may help. It's about praying to have the Spirit with us continually, so that as we read, we can be taught what the Lord wants us to understand, so it will help us in our particular needs, or as in this case, in our relationships.

It isn't about diagramming battle strategies–although there are days that may help. It's about taking the real life problems from our own battlefronts and arming ourselves with "the sword of the Spirit, which is the word of God" (Ephesians 6:17) and fighting for our homes and liberty, our spouses, and our children (see Alma 43:45).

It isn't about speeding through the scriptures at a break-neck pace to meet some deadline—although there may be times when that may help. It's about noticing those times that we don't want to move, or breathe, for fear of dislodging the feeling that has come upon us as the Spirit opens our under-standing to something we may have never before considered.

It's not just about taking copious notes when we read— although that may help. It's about noting which words and phrases are being inscribed "in [the] fleshy tables of [our] heart[s]" (2 Corinthians 3:3).

It's not just about learning more about the Savior's life— although that may help. It's about coming to know the Savior and binding ourselves to Him in ways we never have before.

It's not just about learning names and dates and places— although that may help. It's about learning to take upon us the name of Christ in a whole new way.

It's not just about reading the scriptures. It's about learning to hear the voice of the Lord.

And, really, it's not just about loving the scriptures, although our love for them will increase our ability to give and receive love. It's ALL about our love for the Lord, The Rock, upon Whom, if we build our relationships, we cannot fall.

THERE IS NO END

Therefore, the conclusion to this book is that there is no end—no end to the wisdom to be found in the scriptures. In His precious word, the Lord has given us an inexhaustible store of inspired teachings—truths that will help us to build *Rock*-solid relationships. "Truly, there is no end to wisdom; . . . there is no end to love" (*Hymns*, no. 284).

*Our minds being now enlightened, we began to have
the scriptures laid open to our understandings, and the true
meaning and intention of their more mysterious passages revealed
unto us in a manner which we never could attain
to previously, nor ever before had thought of.*

—Joseph Smith—History 1:74

REFERENCES

Ballard, Melvin J. "The Sacramental Covenant." *Improvement Era* 22, no. 12 (October 1919): 1025–32.

Cook, Gene R. *Teaching by the Spirit*. Talk on Cassette. Salt Lake City: Deseret Book, 1998.

Dew, Sheri L. *No Doubt About It*. Salt Lake City: Deseret Book, 2001.

Discourses of Brigham Young. Edited by John A. Widtsoe. Salt Lake City: Bookcraft, 1998.

Feinauer, L. L., E. H. Callahan, and H. G. Hilton. "Hardiness as a Moderator of Shame Associated with Childhood Sexual Abuse in Women." *American Journal of Family Therapy* 31: 65–78.

Holland, Jeffrey R. *Of Souls, Symbols, and Sacraments*. Salt Lake City: Deseret Book, 2001.

Hymns of The Church of Jesus Christ of Latter-day Saints. Salt Lake City: The Church of Jesus Christ of Latter-day Saints, 1985.

Kimball, Spencer W. *The Miracle of Forgiveness*. Salt Lake City: Bookcraft, 1969.

Maturana, Humberto R., and Francisco J. Varela. *The Tree of Knowledge: The Biological Roots of Human Understanding*. Rev. ed. Boston: Shambhala, 1992.

Pratt, Parley P. *Key to the Science of Theology*. Salt Lake City: Deseret Book, 1978.

Smith, Joseph. *Teachings of the Prophet Joseph Smith*. Compiled by Joseph Fielding Smith. Salt Lake City: Deseret Book, 1976.

Watson, Wendy L. *Purity and Passion*. Salt Lake City: Deseret Book, 2001.

Wright, Lorraine M., Wendy L. Watson, and Janice M. Bell. *Beliefs: The Heart of Healing in Families and Illness*. New York: BasicBooks, 1996.

INDEX